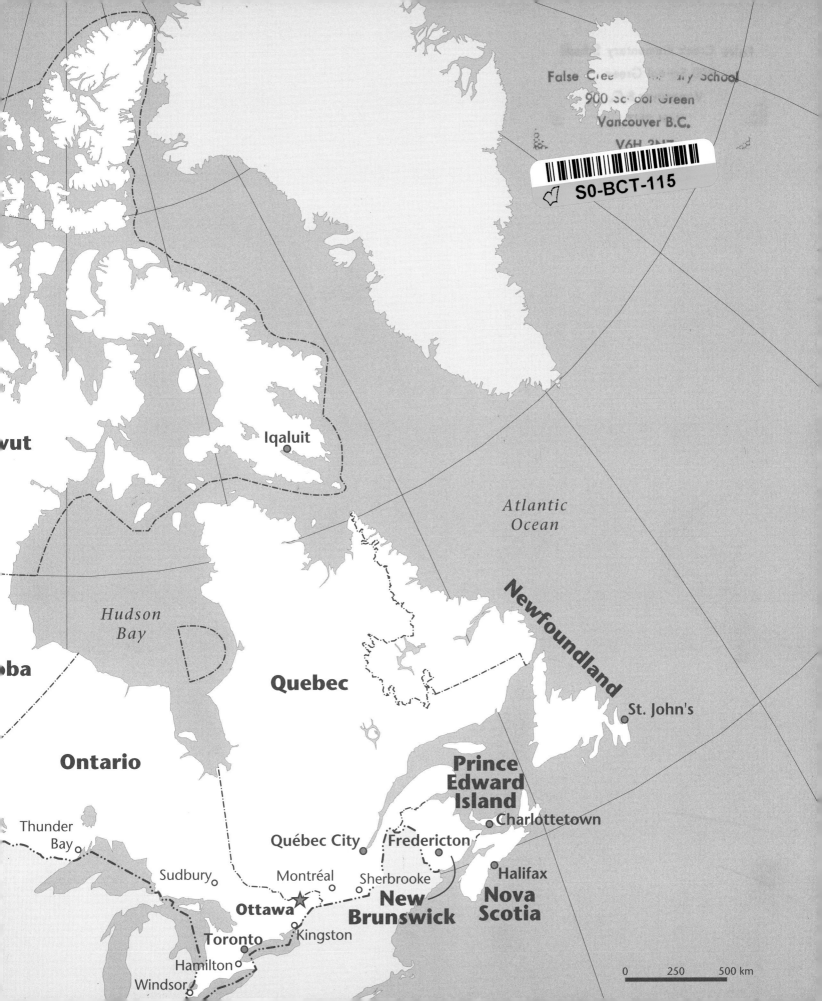

Iqaluit

Atlantic Ocean

Hudson Bay

Newfoundland

Quebec

St. John's

Ontario

Prince Edward Island

ba

vut

Charlottetown

Thunder Bay

Québec City

Fredericton

Sudbury

Montréal

Sherbrooke

Halifax

Ottawa

New Brunswick

Nova Scotia

Kingston

Toronto

Hamilton

Windsor

0   250   500 km

False Creek Elementary School
900 School Green
Vancouver B.C.
V6H 3N7

Connections Canada

OUTLOOKS **5**

DANIEL FRANCIS

Cover Art:
Emily Carr, *Abstract Tree Forms,* VAG 42.3.54
Vancouver Art Gallery/Trevor Mills

OXFORD
UNIVERSITY PRESS

OXFORD
UNIVERSITY PRESS

70 Wynford Drive, Don Mills, Ontario M3C 1J9
www.oup.com/ca

Oxford New York

Auckland   Bangkok   Buenos Aires   Cape Town   Chennai
Dar es Salaam   Delhi   Hong Kong   Istanbul   Karachi   Kolkata
Kuala Lumpur   Madrid   Melbourne   Mexico City   Mumbai   Nairobi
São Paulo   Shanghai   Singapore   Taipei   Tokyo   Toronto

with an associated company in Berlin

Oxford is a trade mark of Oxford University Press
in the UK and in certain other countries

Published in Canada
By Oxford University Press

Canadian Cataloguing in Publication Data

Francis, Daniel
  Connections Canada
(Outlooks ; 5)
For use in grade 5.
Includes index.
ISBN 0-19-541429-2

1. Canada — History — Juvenile literature. I. Title. II. Series.

FC170.F72 2000   971   C99-932831-X
F1026.F68 2000

6 7 8 – 03 02

This book is printed on permanent (acid-free) paper ∞.

Printed in Canada

Contents

Acknowledgements

The author and the publisher wish to thank Sharon Sterling and Arnold Toutant for their guidance and advice, and Rosemary Neering for her contribution to the development of the manuscript.

The author and the publisher also extend their thanks to the following people for reviewing the manuscript:

Donna Anderson
Coal Tyee Elementary School
Nanaimo, BC

Sheila Borman
Kitchener Elementary School
Burnaby, BC

Judy Dallin
Coordinator of Aboriginal Programs
Langley, BC

Pat Horstead
Maple Ridge Primary School
Maple Ridge, BC

Credits

Cover Design: Tearney McMurtry

Text Design: Brett Miller

Layout: Linda Mackey

Cartographic Art: Dave McKay

Illustrations: Heather Graham

Cover Image: Emily Carr, *Abstract Tree Forms*, VAG 42.3.54, Vancouver Art Gallery/Trevor Mills

Introduction

Connections Canada is a social studies textbook about you and your community.

In grade 4 social studies, you learned about what life was like for Canada's Aboriginal peoples. You also found out about the first explorers who came to Canada from Europe and how these two groups got along.

Connections Canada is also about the past. You can discover how people from all over the world made Canada their home. You can learn about the kind of society they created in Canada and how they used resources to build their communities.

Learning about the past tells us much about our own time. It helps us to understand how the world we live in came to be the way it is. By learning about how things changed in the past, we can prepare to deal with changes in our own lives.

Connections Canada can help you learn about your community and how to make it a better place in which to live. Everyone of us has something unique to give. You *can* make a difference.

Chapter 1

Coming Together

People have come to live in Canada from many other countries around the world. Think of your own classroom. Were some of your classmates born in other countries? Even if they were born in Canada, many students have parents or grandparents who came here from somewhere else.

The First Nations people and the Inuit say that their **ancestors** have lived here since before anyone can remember. (Ancestors are people from whom we are descended.) The parents or ancestors of other Canadians chose to move here from various places. In this way, Canada is a country of newcomers.

What about yourself? Where were you born—in Canada or elsewhere? When did members of your family move to Canada?

In this chapter, you can learn about the **diversity** [dih-VUR-suh-tee] of Canada. What do you think *diversity* means? As you read through the chapter, you can build on your understanding. Think about the things that make parts of the country different from each other. You'll discover the great variety of people who call themselves Canadians.

A Country of Many Differences

Have you ever travelled across Canada? If you have, then you have seen what a huge country it is. Canada stretches from the Atlantic to the Pacific Oceans and all the way to the North Pole. Measured by area, it is the second largest country in the world.

It is not surprising that such a big place is also very diverse. There are many different kinds of landscape and climate. The mountains of British Columbia, the flat prairies of Saskatchewan, the rocky Shield country of northern Ontario, the frozen tundra of the North, the fertile farmland along the St. Lawrence River—these are all part of Canada.

Reading a Map

Different kinds of maps contain different kinds of information. When you need to figure out how to go somewhere, you sometimes use a street map to plan your route. Highway maps show the roads leading from one community to another. A map of the world might give the names of all the countries and their capital cities.

The map on pages 4 and 5 contains a different kind of information. It is called a **relief map**. Even though it is drawn on a flat surface, it uses colour to show how the land surface becomes higher or lower. Brown is the colour used to show high, mountainous country. Dark green is used to show low land that lies very close to the level of the ocean.

The colours are a kind of code. Once you understand the code, you can tell which parts of Canada have very high land and which parts are low lying. For instance, on this map, you can see that the middle of Quebec is more mountainous than the rest of the province.

Reading Hint

When you see a word in **boldface**, it is important to add this word to your vocabulary. The meaning of the word will be explained nearby or in the same sentence. Sometimes you will be asked to give your own definition of a boldface word.

ARCTIC
OCEAN

Beaufort Sea

Prince
Patrick
Island

Sver
Isla

Queen Elizab

Banks
Island

Melville
Island

Prince
of Wales
Island

Victoria Island

Gulf
of
Alaska

PACIFIC
OCEAN

Yukon R.

Mackenzie Mountains

Mackenzie R.

Liard

Great
Bear
Lake

Great Slave Lake

Mt. Logan
5951 m

Western Cordillera

Rocky Mountains

Interior

Queen
Charlotte
Islands

Coast Mountains

Peace River

Lake Athabasca

Canad

Mt. Robson
3954 m

Athabasca River

Churchill R.

Nelson River

Mt. Waddington
3994 m

Vancouver Island

Yellowhead
Pass

North

Saskatchewan River

Lake
Winnipeg

CA

Kicking Horse
Pass

South

Lake
Winnipegosis

P
l
a
i
n
s

Columbia R.

Crowsnest
Pass

Lake o
the W

USA

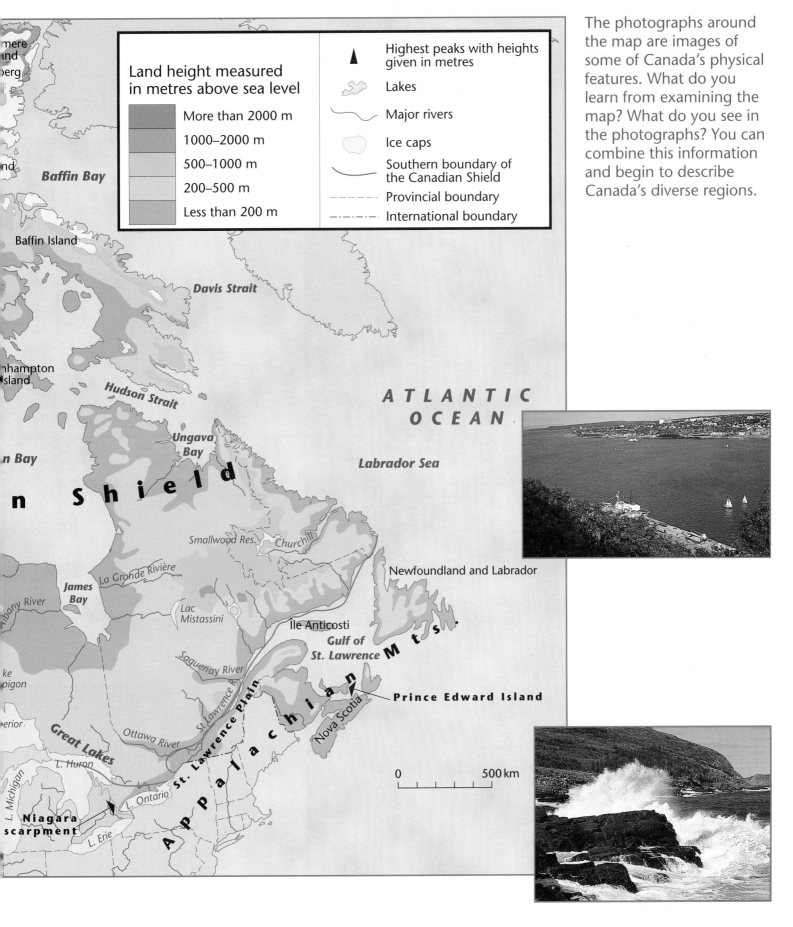

Land height measured
in metres above sea level

More than 2000 m
1000–2000 m
500–1000 m
200–500 m
Less than 200 m

Highest peaks with heights
given in metres

Lakes

Major rivers

Ice caps

Southern boundary of
the Canadian Shield

Provincial boundary

International boundary

Baffin Bay

Baffin Island

Davis Strait

nhampton
sland

Hudson Strait

n Bay

Ungava
Bay

n S h i e l d

James
Bay

La Grande Rivière

Smallwood Res.

Churchill

Lac
Mistassini

Île Anticosti

Saguenay River

St Lawrence R.

Ottawa River

St. Lawrence Plain

Great Lakes

L. Huron

L. Ontario

Niagara
scarpment

L. Erie

Albany River

ke
pigon

erior

L. Michigan

ATLANTIC
OCEAN

Labrador Sea

Newfoundland and Labrador

Gulf of
St. Lawrence   M t s .

A p p a l a c h i a n

Nova Scotia

Prince Edward Island

0   500 km

The photographs around
the map are images of
some of Canada's physical
features. What do you
learn from examining the
map? What do you see in
the photographs? You can
combine this information
and begin to describe
Canada's diverse regions.

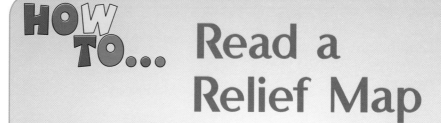

HOW TO... Read a Relief Map

A relief map uses a colour code. You can break this code by looking at the legend, or key. This tells you what the colours on the map mean.

The colours on the map show how high the land is. The height of land is measured by its distance above sea level. Land at sea level is 0 metres.

By reading the key, you will discover which parts of Canada are the highest and which parts are the lowest.

Try This

Take another look at the relief map on pages 4 and 5. You can answer these questions by breaking the colour code.

- *What part of Canada seems to be the highest?*

- *Find your community on the map. What is its elevation? Is your community higher or lower than Winnipeg, Manitoba? than Halifax, Nova Scotia?*

- *In the spring of the year, as the snow melts, the rivers fill with water and become rushing torrents. Looking at the map, can you tell which areas might be at risk from flooding?*

In The Words Of...

Nils

Nils Anderson is 12 years old. He lives in Nelson, a city on Kootenay Lake in British Columbia. Here he describes the landscape and climate and his favourite activities.

There are rounded mountains here with lots of **conifers** [KON-uh-furz] and also lots of craggy, snow-topped mountains. There are a lot of beaches and many creeks. The lake is about 150 metres deep. Even in the summer it stays pretty cold, but you get used to it once you are numb. Sometimes, the lake is so smooth it is like a mirror of the mountains. Bad storms can come up the valley very fast. We started on a canoe trip across the lake one sunny day, and halfway across a big storm blew in and just about capsized us. Boy, did we paddle fast!

In winter, it gets to about –10 degrees Celsius and we get up to 1 metre of snow. In the summer, it can get to 30 degrees Celsius with lots of sun, but we live on the side of a mountain so we almost always have a gentle breeze.

I like to swim, ski, hike, fish, bike, beachcomb, and paddle around our ponds in a little kayak. A day spent outdoors, I would probably paddle around in the boats and try some fishing for perch in the ponds. Or, I might wander in the fields and woods until I thought of something neat to do. When I bike to school, the kilometre down the side of our mountain is fun, but when I come home, it is hard work.

We live on 40 hectares of farmland and forest on the side of a mountain. We can see the Milky Way, the Northern Lights, and lots of shooting stars. Special things like satellites and comets are clear too.

We have lots of wildlife, even in our own backyard. There are elk, moose, mule and white-tailed deer, waterfowl, songbirds, cougars, black bears, sometimes a grizzly, osprey, bald eagles, hawks, owls, lizards, turtles, snakes, and lots of rodents. The Canada geese tried hard to land and make a nest on the metal roof of our house. It sounded like Santa's reindeer trying to land. In winter, we don't have much snow at our house, but the mountains always have lots for cross-country and downhill skiing and snowboarding. We snowshoe and toboggan and ice-fish at our place. Some mornings I get up at 4 a.m. so we can fish for Dolly Varden and kokanee. I usually catch enough for a meal. Yum! Once I caught a 4-kilogram Dolly.

I like the mountains. We have everything here except flatland like the prairies, but we can always go visit relatives there. The advertising says Nelson is the best-kept secret—it is just *perfect*.

Reprinted by permission.

Try This

Nils gives his impression of his part of Canada. How would you describe your part of Canada?

Think about the climate, the landscape, and the kinds of activities that go on there. You might want to write your own brief description of the place where you live. You could start by making a list of three or four key words that you would use. Or, you may want to draw a picture showing your community and the things that make it special.

What Is Your Canada Like?

If you asked students in Newfoundland this question, they might say that Canada is a rocky land, close to the ocean, where people fish for a living. If you asked students in Saskatchewan, they might say that it is a flat land, with huge, open skies, where most people farm for a living. In his own way, Nils has also answered this question as well.

All these answers are correct. There are many Canadas, and each one has its own landscape and character.

Try This

Create a Canada scrapbook that shows the diversity of the country. Collect photographs of different parts of Canada. Magazines and newspapers are good sources of information.

Canada is often divided into five regions: Atlantic Canada, Central Canada, the Prairies, the North, and British Columbia. Locate each region on the map on pages 4 and 5.

Try to find three or four images that show each of the different regions. Divide your scrapbook into chapters, so that each chapter looks at a different region of Canada. Paste the images into your scrapbook. Identify the features that help you to tell one region from another.

O Canada

The **national anthem** of Canada is *O Canada*. Do you know the words? Without looking at the words of the anthem, try writing them out. Now compare your version to the actual words shown on this page. Were you close?

The first line of the anthem is, "O Canada, our home and native land." Your **native land** means the land where you were born. For many Canadians, though, Canada is not their native land. They were not born here. Some were born in another country and came as children with their parents to live in Canada. Others came here as grownups. This is another way in which Canada is a diverse country. Canadians have come from many different places to their new home in Canada.

Citizenship and Heritage Week

O Canada

O Canada!

Our home and native land!

True patriot love in all
thy sons command.

With glowing hearts
we see thee rise,

The True North strong
and free!

From far and wide,
O Canada,

We stand on guard for thee.

God keep our land
glorious and free!

O Canada, we stand
on guard for thee.

O Canada, we stand
on guard for thee.

Government of Canada   Gouvernement du Canada   Canada

A **national anthem** is a song that expresses a strong feeling about a country. Make a list of the words in the anthem that describe Canada. What feelings do these words express?

Cultural Origin	Per Cent
Canadian	31.0
English	24.0
French	20.0
Scottish	15.0
Irish	13.0
German	10.0
Italian	4.0
Aboriginal	4.0
Ukrainian	3.5
Chinese	3.0
Dutch	3.0
Polish	3.0
South Asian	2.5
Jewish	1.0
Norwegian	1.0

Counting Canadians

Every five years, the government carries out a **census** of all Canadians. A census is a count of how many people are living in the country. Census forms collect all kinds of other information as well. For each household, the census asks about the number of people that live there, what their jobs are, what religions they hold, what level of education they have, and so on. This allows the government to understand how the population of Canada is growing and changing.

If you were asked the question, how would you describe your cultural origin? If you were born someplace else, then came to Canada with your family, you could reply with the country of your birth. If your mother is Canadian and your father is Japanese, you could say that you are Canadian, Japanese, or Japanese Canadian. And what about your grandparents? Where

The census that was carried out in 1996 showed that Canada had a population of 29.6 million people. It also showed that these people came from many different backgrounds. When asked what their **cultural origin** was, Canadians gave many different answers. This chart shows the top 15 answers.

did they come from? If they came to Canada from Ireland, you could say that your cultural background is Irish. Finally, you could simply say that you are Canadian.

Trying to put cultural labels on people is complicated, isn't it? But it does show how diverse the population of Canada is. It is a country of many cultures, and all of them play an important role in making Canada what it is today.

Cultural origin refers to the country from which your family or ancestors came.

Another word used to describe your cultural background is **heritage.** Your heritage is all the different cultures of your family.

 **Make a Graph**

A graph is a way of displaying information as a picture. For example, say you had a basket of fruit containing four apples, two pears, and two peaches. What per cent of the basket is made up of each fruit?

To answer this question, you can take a picture of a circle and divide it up as shown below.

The result is a circle graph. It shows that one-half of the basket is apples, one-quarter is pears, and the other quarter is peaches.

Another way to answer this question is to draw a bar graph. The **vertical line** shows the per cent of the basket. Each bar along the **horizontal line** represents a fruit.

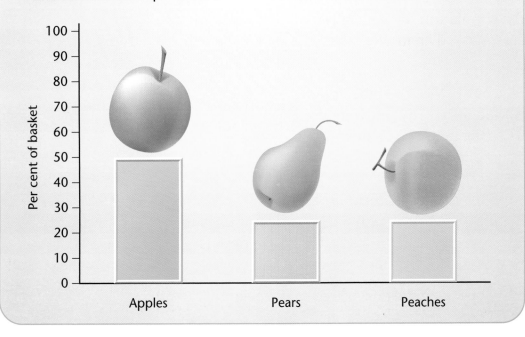

The census information on page 10 is displayed in a chart. You can also display this information in a bar graph.

- Draw the horizontal and vertical lines of the graph. To guide you, look at the bar graph on page 11.

- Along the vertical line, show the per cent of the population. Write 0 at the bottom, then 10, 20, 30, and so on, until you reach 100.

- Along the horizontal line, show each of the 15 cultural origins. For each cultural origin, draw a bar to show what per cent of the population it is. For example, to show the per cent of people of French cultural origin, draw a bar that extends to 20. Remember to label each of the bars.

Find Out

A census is a kind of **survey**. A survey is a way of gathering information about a subject. Carry out a census of your class. Make up a census form asking five basic questions.

- *How old are you?*

- *What is your cultural background?*

- *What language do you speak at home?*

- *Do you follow a religion? If so, which one?*

- *How long have you lived in this neighbourhood?*

The result gives you a way of describing the class. It will tell you

- the number of students in the class

- their ages

- their cultural backgrounds

- the languages they speak

- the religions they follow

- how long they have lived in the neighbourhood

The census will reveal how much diversity there is in your class.

Painting Canada

When Nils was asked to talk about his part of Canada, he began by describing the land. He said that his hometown of Nelson was surrounded by high mountains. Perhaps you began the same way when you described the place where you live. It is a natural place to begin. It is something like being an artist and painting a picture with words.

Artists are often the people we turn to when we want to express our ideas about what kind of place Canada is. Artists paint many things, of course. Some of them paint portraits of people. Some paint shapes and colours that have their own beauty, but do not look like objects in the real world. And some paint images of the landscape.

During the 1920s, there was a group of painters in Toronto known as the Group of Seven. These painters dedicated themselves to painting the Canadian landscape. They packed up their brushes and paints and travelled into the northern woods like explorers. They used bright colours and swirling brush strokes

J. E. H. MacDonald was one of the Group of Seven. This painting, called *The Solemn Land*, is a scene in northern Ontario. What season of the year do you think it is? What are the features that make this scene noticeably Canadian?

to show the wildness of the land. "We believe wholeheartedly in the land," they declared.

No one had ever painted Canada like this before. But soon the Group of Seven was very popular. Today, they are probably the most famous painters Canada has ever produced.

REAL PEOPLE: EMILY CARR

At the same time as the Group of Seven were painting Ontario, another painter was busy on the coast of British Columbia. She was Emily Carr, an artist from Victoria on Vancouver Island.

Emily Carr lived from 1871 to 1945. She struggled to be an artist. When she was starting out, there was not much interest in art in British Columbia. No one wanted to buy her paintings and she got very little support. For many years, she gave up painting because she had to make a living as a boarding-house keeper.

But Emily Carr managed to return to painting. She travelled up and down the coast of British Columbia painting the Aboriginal villages and the deep forest that surrounded them. Today, the art school in Vancouver is named after her.

In all her work, Emily Carr was trying to express what she called "a British Columbia way of seeing." What do you think she meant by that?

This painting by Emily Carr is called *Big Raven*. The raven was a sacred animal to the Aboriginal peoples on the West Coast. Carr often painted Aboriginal buildings and wooden carvings. Imagine for a moment that you are an artist who wants to paint a picture of the West Coast. What scene would you paint?

Try This

Paintings by the Group of Seven are considered to be typically Canadian. What things do you think of when you hear the word *Canadian*?

Complete the following sentence: *As Canadian as . . .*

Think For Yourself

At the beginning of this chapter, you were asked to define the meaning of the word *diversity*. Now that you have read the chapter, has your definition changed? What is your new definition?

It is time to think critically about diversity. What are some advantages to living in a diverse society? Are there disadvantages? If so, what are they?

Looking Back

In this chapter, you looked at the different regions of Canada. You also learned about the many diverse groups of people who call themselves Canadians.

How do you think that knowing about different parts of the country might help you to understand it better?

Chapter 2

Canada's Founding Peoples

Founding peoples is a term used to describe the earliest communities in a country. They are the first groups to live in a certain place. Therefore, they have a strong influence on the type of society that develops there.

Canada has three founding peoples. From the earliest times, the land was occupied by its original inhabitants, the First Nations and the Inuit [IN-yoo-it] of the Arctic region. Hundreds of years ago, French people began arriving from Europe and settling along the St. Lawrence River. The French were followed by newcomers from Great Britain. Over the years, these three founding peoples combined to create a unique society in the territory that came to be called Canada.

In this chapter, you can learn about the earliest communities in Canada. As you discover their influence in shaping Canadian society, think about why it is important to respect the contributions of people who lived in Canada a long time ago.

The First Peoples

First Nations and Inuit have been living in North America for as long as anyone can remember. They are the original inhabitants of the territory we now call Canada.

Can you imagine what it was like to be the first people? This was long before the time of modern technology. There were no cities, no highways or automobiles, and no factories or mines. Thundering herds of buffalo still stampeded across the Plains. The lakes were filled with fish, and the forests were filled with wild animals.

The people made their living from the land. They built their houses out of wood from the trees or from the skins of animals. They made clothing from woven bark or from furs and tanned animal hides. They obtained food by hunting for deer, buffalo, and other animals, by fishing in the lakes and rivers, and by gathering wild plants.

In the Arctic, the Copper Inuit hunted seals. On the Pacific Coast, the Nuu-chah-nulth [noo-CHAH-noolth] harpooned whales. In Eastern Canada, the Haudenosaunee [ha-duh-nuh-SAH-nee] raised crops of corn. Each part of the country provided its own way of making a living.

In the past, the Haudenosaunee were called the Iroquois [IR-uh-kwah].

Aboriginal peoples living on the Plains hunted the buffalo on horseback. They also drove them over cliffs or chased them into pens. The meat was used for food, and the skins and bones for making tools and utensils.

A Closer Look

Origins of the First Peoples

Every Aboriginal group in Canada has its own creation story. A creation story is a story that explains how the world began and where the first people came from.

Here is a creation story from the Haida [HY-duh] who live on the Queen Charlotte Islands in British Columbia. The story was told by the Haida artist Bill Reid.

One day soon after the great flood the Raven walked upon the beach. The mischievous Raven was bored. In frustration he complained to the empty sky. To his delight he heard a muffled squeak.

Right at his feet was a huge clamshell. He looked more closely and saw that it was full of little creatures.

Well, here was something to break the monotony [a lack of variety] of his day. But it wasn't much fun as long as the silly things stayed in their shell. So he leaned his great head close, and used his bell-like crooning voice to coax them to come out and play in the wonderful shining world. First one, then another of the shell dwellers clambered out, as curiosity overcame caution. These were the original Haidas, the first humans.

Excerpt from *Raven Steals the Light* copyright © 1988 by Bill Reid and Robert Bringhurst. Published in Canada by Douglas & Mcintyre. Reprinted by permission of the publisher.

A Different Understanding

Europeans who came to live in Canada developed their own understanding of how humans first came to America. They believed that the first people walked across the Bering Strait into America from Siberia. This happened many thousands of years ago, when the Bering Strait was dry land. (See the map on page 19.)

No matter which story you believe, both recognize that the First Nations and Inuit lived in America long before anyone else arrived.

This huge sculpture by Bill Reid is called *The Raven and the First Men*. It is on display at the Museum of Anthropology at the University of British Columbia. The sculpture illustrates the creation story.

Find Out

The Haida story is one of many Aboriginal creation stories. You can find more creation stories in the library. Look for books about other Aboriginal groups in Canada. Another source of information might be an Aboriginal Elder. Some students may know stories that are told in their communities.

Write down the details of one of these stories. Bring it to class to share with your classmates. You may want to illustrate the story with a drawing.

Discuss how it is different from the Haida story about Raven and the "clam people." What things do the stories share? Do you believe that the events of the story actually took place? Why or why not?

Why do you think it is important to know that the First Nations and Inuit were the first inhabitants of Canada?

Bering Strait is a narrow sea passage that separates the eastern tip of Russia from Alaska and links the Arctic Ocean with the Bering Sea. During the ice age, the area formed a bridge of land between the two continents.

Using the Right Name

Your name is a way of identifying yourself. It is an important part of who you are. You don't like it when someone says your name incorrectly or mixes you up with someone else.

In the past, Aboriginal groups were given names that did not belong to them. They were not the names used by the peoples themselves.

Take, for example, the Inuit of the Far North. For a long time, non-Inuit called them Eskimos. The word *Eskimo* means "eaters of raw meat" and was a term used by other Aboriginal groups. The northern people prefer to be called Inuit, a word that means "the people." Today, *Eskimo* is not heard very often.

Another example is the term *Indian*, which European explorers used to refer to the original inhabitants of North and South America. When the explorers first arrived in America, they were lost and thought they were in India. So they called the people living here Indians, but this was a mistake.

The government still uses the word *Indian* to define some Aboriginal peoples under the Indian Act (see pages 89 to 90). In general, though, it has been replaced by the term **Aboriginal peoples**. *Aboriginal peoples* means the original inhabitants of Canada. It includes Indians, Inuit, and Métis [may-TEE]. **First Nations** refers to organized groups, or nations, of Aboriginal peoples who live in Canada— from the Mi'kmaq in Nova Scotia to the Haida in British Columbia. There are hundreds of First Nations in Canada, each with its own history and traditions, and each with its own local name.

A Closer Look

The Métis

When Europeans began arriving in America, they mixed with the Aboriginal peoples. European men often married Aboriginal women. The children of these marriages were a mixture of both backgrounds. They were known as "mixed bloods," or by a French word, *métis,* meaning a mixture of backgrounds.

The Métis developed their own unique way of life. They worked in the fur trade and specialized in the buffalo hunt on the western Plains. Meat from the hunt was used to feed the traders at the fur posts. The Métis had their own language. It was called *michif* [mee-SHEEF] and was a mixture of Cree, French, and Ojibwa [o-JIB-wah].

The Métis in Western Canada saw themselves as a separate people. They wanted their own homeland where their culture, language, and traditions would be respected. Led by Louis Riel [loo-EE ree-EL], they organized themselves to protect their lands against the European settlers who were moving in.

In the end, the Métis were pushed aside by the newcomers. They lost most of their land. But they survived as a separate people with a proud history. In 1996, the census showed that there were 210 190 Métis living in Canada.

This painting of a Métis man and two women dates from the 1800s. It shows the unique clothing styles that were part of the Métis culture. What influences of European culture do you see in the painting? What influences of Aboriginal culture do you see?

Try This

The term *Aboriginal peoples* includes three groups: First Nations, Inuit, and Métis. How would you compare these groups? In other words, in what ways are they the same and in what ways are they different?

Here's a chart that you can use to make your comparison. Write the main questions in the first column.

If you need more information about any of these groups, do some research in the library.

	First Nations	Inuit	Métis
In what part of Canada do they live?			
How did they find food in the past?			
How did they make clothing in the past?			
What other facts do I know?			

Aboriginal Peoples Today

Aboriginal peoples are still an important part of Canadian society today. There are about 800 000 First Nations, Inuit, and Métis living in communities across Canada. Aboriginal peoples make contributions in every walk of life.

In 1993, John Kim Bell, a famous Mohawk conductor and composer, set up the National Aboriginal Achievement Awards. This annual ceremony honours the achievements of Aboriginal peoples in many fields, including medicine, the arts, and business. For instance, in 1997, a Métis doctor, Martin McLoughlin of Vancouver, received an award for his contribution to medicine.

Think about how often you see evidence of Aboriginal peoples' contributions in our society.

Susan Aglukark [uh-GLOO-kark] is an Inuit and an award-winning singer. Her songs are in English and **Inuktitut** [in-UK-ti-tut], the language of the Inuit.

The French in Canada

The next time you pour yourself a bowl of cereal, be sure to pay attention to the writing on the box. You have probably already noticed that it includes both French and English. But have you ever wondered why?

It is not just cereal boxes that have writing in two languages—so do all kinds of other containers, the labels on clothes, and the signs at the airport. Can you think of other examples?

A Bilingual Country

The writing on cereal boxes, clothing labels, and other items that you found is a sign that Canada is a bilingual country. This means that it has two official languages. An **official language** is one that is used by the government in conducting the business of the nation. Many languages are spoken in Canada, but only two have official status. The two official languages are French and English.

Bilingualism [by-LING-gwal-iz-um] means that Canadians have the right to receive government services in French or English, no matter where they live in the country. Of course, they may carry on their daily lives in any language they choose. No one is forced to speak a certain language. But when dealing with their government, people can expect to receive service in one of the official languages.

French-speaking people live in communities all across Canada. It is common to see French names on the map of Canada. Most of us can watch French-language programs on television or buy French-language books in our communities.

Can you find other signs of bilingualism in your community and in your province?

The singer Céline Dion is probably the most well-known Canadian in the world. Her CDs sell millions of copies, and she has won many awards. Céline Dion is a Québécoise who was born near the city of Montreal. She made her first hit record when she was only 13 years old. She sings and records in both French and English.

The Arrival of the French

How did Canada come to have two official languages?

Almost 500 years ago, explorers came to North America from France. They were seeking new lands and the wealth they hoped to find there. The French built forts and began trading for furs with the Aboriginal peoples.

French explorers travelled far into the interior of the country, looking for new places where they could trade. Soon they declared that they owned the whole region. Settlers arrived to build communities and begin farming. They called this area New France.

New France was a **colony** of France. A colony is a territory that belongs to another country. Great Britain, France, and Spain all had colonies in North America.

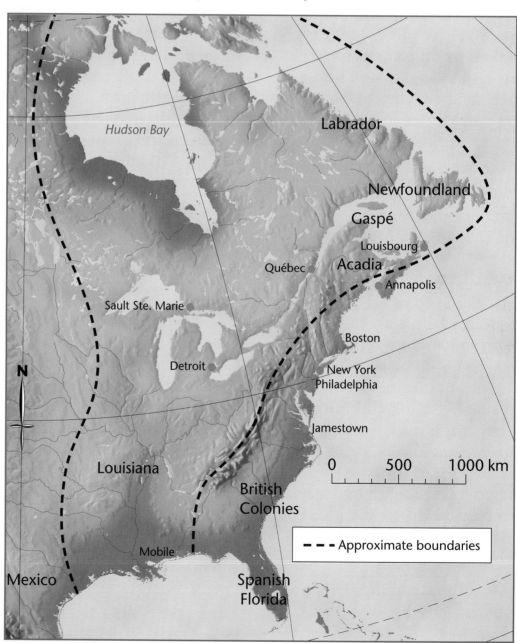

This map shows New France in 1712, when it reached its largest extent. From then on, the area controlled by Britain grew larger, and the area controlled by France shrank until it was roughly the size of the province of Quebec today.

Hudson Bay

Labrador

Newfoundland

Gaspé

Louisbourg

Québec · Acadia

Annapolis

Sault Ste. Marie

Boston

Detroit

New York
Philadelphia

Jamestown

Louisiana

British Colonies

0   500   1000 km

Mobile

Mexico

Spanish Florida

- - - Approximate boundaries

Life in New France

On pages 25 to 27, you will find evidence of the life led by the colonists in New France. As you examine this evidence, create a chart like the one shown here to record your findings:

What did the colonists eat?	How did they get the food they ate?	What were some of the occupations they had?	What hardships did the colonists face?

"The colonist eats two pounds of bread a day and six ounces of bacon."

—Intendant Radot, 1636

"In 1737, the famine was so terrible that colonists were reduced to eating buds of trees, potatoes, and other foods never intended to be used as food for human beings."

—Pehr Kalm, 1753

The colonists of New France were called *habitants* [AB-ee-tah(n)]. This painting shows a *habitant* who has been hunting. Describe his clothing. Which items of clothing do you think were borrowed from the Aboriginal peoples?

This view of Quebec City shows the marketplace and different street activities. It also shows the cathedral.

Type of Craft	Number of Craftspersons
miller	1
baker	16
butcher	18
mason-stonecutter	32
woodworker	42
carpenter	84
roofer	1
chimney sweep	4
shipwright	2
cooper	26
tailor	20
tanner/currier	6
shoemaker	26
saddler	3
blacksmith	30
locksmith	3
armourer/gunsmith	3
silversmith	6
surgeon	6
wigmaker/barber	11

"When a family begins to build a place to live, it needs two or three years before it has enough to feed itself. People also need clothing, furniture, and many little things. When these first difficulties are past, they begin to live comfortably, and may become rich with time. In the beginning, they live on their cereals and vegetables and on wild game, which is plentiful in winter. To get clothing and other things for the house, they make roofing planks and cut timber which they sell at a high price."

—Marie de l'Incarnation, a nun who lived in New France from 1639 to 1672

This chart shows the type and number of craftspeople in Quebec City in 1744. You might have to use your dictionary to find out what some of these crafts are. Which jobs are still done today in your community?

Goods Traded for Furs	Furs Traded
guns	beaver
gunpowder	lynx
hatchets	marten
cloth	fox
kettles	bear
string	otter
knives	wolverine
beads	mink
blankets	wolf
tobacco	

This chart shows the type of goods that the French traded for furs from Aboriginal peoples.

This painting gives a view of the countryside of New France. Why were most farms located next to a river? The white house is the main farmhouse. The plank building on the right is the barn. Do you see the stakes in the river? Those are weirs (a type of trap) for catching fish.

"Fisheries of all kinds are in operation, the rivers being very rich in fish, such as salmon, brill, perch, sturgeon, herring, and cod. They are prepared both fresh and dried, and much is sold in France, which makes us richer. The seal fishery furnishes the whole country and much is sent to France. This year, we are shipping overseas fresh and dried codfish, salted salmon, eels, peas both green and white, fish oil, staves [sticks or poles] and boards, all produced in the country."

—A letter from a Jesuit priest

Try This

Look at the variety of information on pages 25 to 27. Some of it is contained in charts. Some of it can be found in the photographs. Using all the information, make a list of the goods that were exported from New France to Europe. List the items they imported from France. What important items did the colonists produce for themselves?

Items Exported to France	Items Imported from France	Items Produced for Themselves

Imagine that you are a colonist living in New France. How would you prefer to make your living? Send a letter home to France, explaining your decision.

The French Presence Today

A **first language** is the language that a person first learns at home.

Eventually, France lost control of its colony in North America. New France became a possession of Great Britain and became known as Quebec. But French-speaking people continued to live in Quebec and to play an important role in the development of Canada.

There are many ways in which Canada's French heritage lives on in Canada. Today, one Canadian in five traces his or her ancestry back to France. One in four speaks French as a **first language**. All across the country, students learn French as a second language.

The ancestors of these Acadian dancers in Prince Edward Island came from France.

The British in Canada

If you take some coins out of your pocket and spread them on the desk, what images do you see? Canadian coins are decorated with pictures of different animals. There is an elk, a beaver, and a polar bear on the two-dollar coin (if you are lucky enough to have one of those!). And on the reverse side of every coin there is a portrait of Queen Elizabeth II.

Have you ever wondered why the image of the queen is so common in Canada? She is also pictured on all our paper money and on some stamps. Her portrait hangs in many public buildings. There is probably a picture of the queen hanging in your school.

Queen Elizabeth II is the queen of England, and she is also the queen of Canada. This means that Canada is a **monarchy**. In the old days, a monarch (a king or queen) had absolute power to do whatever he or she chose. Today, the role of the monarch is mainly ceremonial (for the sake of tradition). Government is carried on by elected parliaments, not by monarchs.

Still, the queen is an important person in our system of government. All the laws are passed in her name. She has her own representative in Canada, called the **governor general**. The governor general carries out many duties on behalf of the queen.

The monarchy is one sign of how important British traditions are in Canada.

Queen Elizabeth II has reigned since 1952. When she dies, or steps aside, her eldest son Charles, the Prince of Wales, will become king. Both Queen Elizabeth and Prince Charles have made several visits to Canada.

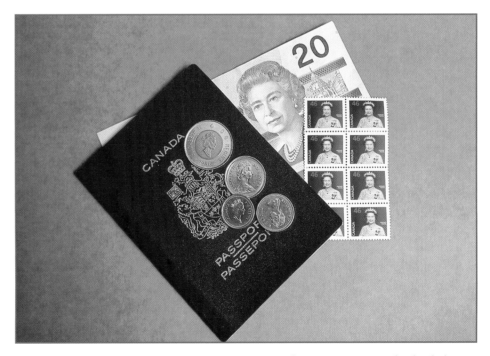

The queen's image on stamps, coins, and so on is a symbol of the monarchy in Canada.

Think For Yourself

The images that appear on Canadian coins and stamps are important symbols of our society. They represent our pride in our country. What symbol is on the Canadian flag? What does this symbol say about the country? As a class, talk about the role symbols play in society.

Create your own symbol for Canada. Working with a partner, decide on a symbol. Then explain to the rest of the class what you want your symbol to say about the country.

Draw a stamp or coin that illustrates your symbol.

Great Britain is made up of four countries—England, Scotland, Wales, and Northern Ireland—that joined together 200 years ago. They are sometimes simply called Britain or the United Kingdom.

Migrating to Canada

Before 1763 Canada was a French colony. France and Great Britain were rivals for power and wealth around the world. In many places, their competition brought them into conflict. Their rivalry came to a head in the Seven Years War, which lasted from 1756 to 1763. During this long war, British troops came to Canada and drove out the French. In 1763, France signed the Treaty of Paris giving Canada to the British.

With Canada in British hands, many people from Scotland, Ireland, and England began crossing the Atlantic Ocean to live here. Scots were attracted to Nova Scotia in particular. Between 1800 and 1815, there were 10 000 new arrivals in Nova Scotia from Scotland. One popular place for the newcomers to settle was in Cape Breton Island, where the rugged hills and the sea reminded them of home. Today, Gaelic [GALE-ik] (a language spoken in Scotland) is still used there, and Cape Breton Island is known as a centre of Scottish music in North America.

Irish newcomers preferred to settle in Ontario. The Irish were driven from their country by a terrible famine. They arrived in Canada poor and starving. They found jobs in the logging camps or in construction, building roads and canals. By 1871, almost one-quarter of all Canadians were of Irish origin.

During the 19th century, by far the largest number of immigrants to Canada came from Great Britain. As a result, Canadians of British background became the largest group in the country. They joined with the earlier French colonists to be one of Canada's founding peoples.

The British Presence Today

Canada is much less British today than it was 50 or 100 years ago. Newcomers from around the world have arrived to transform Canadian society into a mix of many cultures.

Still, the British heritage is evident in many ways, for example, in our type of government. Our systems of Parliament and elections are modelled on the British systems. So is our system of courts and law. The fact that English is one of the official languages of Canada is another example of British influence. Three Canadians out of every five learn English before any other language.

Can you think of other examples of British heritage in your community?

The Stratford Festival takes place each year from May to October in Stratford, Ontario. This theatre festival, which began in 1953, is another example of Canada's British heritage. The festival puts on plays mostly by the English playwright William Shakespeare. It is modelled on a similar drama festival in Stratford-upon-Avon, Shakespeare's birthplace in England.

Think For Yourself

You have learned that three groups of people have had a deep effect on the development of Canada.

In a group, make a brainstorming web, similar to the one shown here, for each of the founding peoples.

Brainstorm the contributions each of the three groups has made to Canada. Record them in your web.

Art (masks, sculptures, etc.)

Aboriginal peoples

Looking Back

In this chapter, you learned about Canada's three founding peoples. You saw how Aboriginal, French, and British peoples have all made contributions to the kind of place Canada is today.

Why do you think it is important to respect the contributions made by people who lived in Canada a long time ago?

Chapter 3

Coming to Canada

*T*he story of Canada is the story of its people. Aboriginal peoples have been living here for thousands of years. Over the past 400 years, other people have come from all over the world to make their homes in Canada.

Canada is often called a nation of immigrants. Do you recall what the word *immigrant* means? What is a nation of immigrants? Is it an accurate way of describing Canada?

In this chapter, you can learn about the history of immigration to Canada. You'll meet some of the groups of people who came here from other places. As you read the chapter, think about the contributions each of these groups has made to Canadian society.

Making a New Home

When people leave one country and go to live in another, this is known as **emigration**. People have many reasons for emigrating.

Sometimes they are unhappy with living conditions in their own country. They may not be able to buy land. Perhaps they are very poor and have no chance to make things better for themselves. There may be war in their country or some natural disaster that has destroyed their home. Sometimes the government doesn't allow them to practise their religion or to live freely.

These are all reasons that *push* people to leave their home country. They are the **push factors** that lead to emigration.

There are other reasons for moving, which are linked to the benefits offered by living in another country. When people arrive in another country to live, this is called **immigration**. Perhaps the cost of land is cheaper. There may be more jobs and a better chance of making a living. The new country is probably at peace or has a form of government that offers more freedom.

These are the factors that *pull* people toward a new home. They are the **pull factors** that lead to immigration.

These children and their families immigrated to Canada from Great Britain in the early part of the 20th century.

In The Words Of...

Hannah and Nicholas

Children can be immigrants too. Often, young people come with their families to settle in Canada.

*Here is an account by a young immigrant, Hannah Ingraham, who came to live in Canada from the United States in 1783. Her family was escaping the **American Revolution** that was raging in the US. They sailed from New York City, with all their possessions, to live in Nova Scotia.*

I was just 11 years old when we left our farm to come here. It was the last ship of the season and had on board all those who could not come sooner. There were no deaths on board, but several babies were born.

It was a sad, sick time after we landed in Saint John. We had to live in tents. The government gave them to us, and food too. It was just at the first snow. The melting snow and rain would soak up into our beds as we lay.

We lived in a tent until father got a house ready. He went up through our lot till he found a nice fresh spring of water. He stooped down and pulled away the fallen leaves and tasted it. It was very good, so there he built his house. We all had food given to us by the government—flour, butter, and pork. Tools were given to the men also.

Excerpt from Mary Archibald, ed., *United Empire Loyalists: Loyalists of the American Revolution* (Toronto: Dundurn Press, 1978).

Nicholas Hryhorczuk [hre-HOR-chook] came to live in Manitoba with his parents in 1897, when he was nine years old. The family came from the Ukraine [yoo-KRANE], then a part of Austria-Hungary. Years later he recalled what it was like for his family to settle in a new home.

After a 10-day voyage across the Atlantic, we arrived in Halifax and from there we travelled by the immigrant train to Winnipeg. Before many days passed, we were in Dauphin [DAH-fin] to select a **homestead**.

That was our homestead, where my father erected a temporary shelter for our family. It was a large hut which looked like a garage or a root cellar that one sees in some farmyards today.

We spent the summer in this hut, and when it rained the roof would leak. Several times during heavy rains, the water also came in at the ground level and our belongings got wet. However, we did not have many things as two of our trunks which carried Mother's linen and our best clothing had been lost.

Our greatest problem was that we did not have a cow. We were lucky to be able to buy milk from our neighbours. The river helped, too, as we were able to catch some fish in it. Of course, we brought such staples as flour, cornmeal and salt, sugar, lard and tea, with us. We bought a few hens that supplied us with eggs. During the summer, mushrooms and wild berries grew in profusion [plentifully].

Excerpt from *Reflections and Reminiscences: Ukrainians in Canada 1892–1992* by Michael Ewanchuk (Winnipeg: Michael Ewanchuk, 1995), 18–19. Reprinted by permission of Michael Ewanchuk.

The **American Revolution** (1775–1783) was a war between Great Britain and the American Colonies, which belonged to Britain. The colonists did not like being ruled from a distance. They wanted their independence. After they won their independence, the colonies became the United States of America. Many Americans disagreed with the war and wanted to remain loyal to Britain, so they came north to Canada. Hannah Ingraham's family belonged to this **Loyalist** group.

A **homestead** was a piece of land claimed by immigrant settlers for farming.

Try This

Compare Hannah's and Nicholas's experiences of immigration. Look for the ways that their experiences were the same and the ways they were different. Remember that it helps to write down the main ideas so that you record the same type of information for both accounts.

Here's a chart you could use to compare Hannah's and Nicholas's accounts. The main ideas go in the middle boxes.

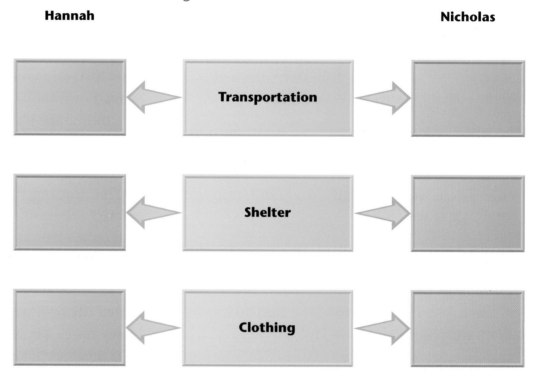

Hannah   Nicholas

Transportation

Shelter

Clothing

Think For Yourself

Imagine that your family has decided to move to another country. You are asked to give your opinion. This means that you will have to think about what will happen if you make one choice or another. Think of the **pros** (good things) and **cons** (bad things) for each choice. List them in a chart like the one shown here.

Pros	Cons

Families settling on a homestead had many chores to do. Even young children helped out.

Black People in Canada

Many Americans opposed the slave laws in their country. They helped the escaped slaves on their flight to Canada by providing food and shelter and smuggling them from place to place in wagons or on boats. Although it was not an actual rail line, this escape network was called the **Underground Railroad**.

The story of immigration to Canada goes back many years. As you read in the last chapter, the earliest immigrants were the colonists in New France. They began arriving in the early 1600s.

The French were followed by other newcomers from all over the world.

Black People in Nova Scotia

Black people have been living in Canada for hundreds of years. The first reported Black man in Canada was Mathieu Da Costa. He served as a translator between the Mi'kmaq and the French at Port-Royal, Nova Scotia, which was founded in 1605.

As the years passed more Black people arrived, mainly from the United States. During the American Revolution, one out of every ten Loyalists who came to Nova Scotia was Black. Today, their ancestors still live in that province.

The Underground Railroad

Most Black people living in the United States in the early days were **slaves**. They were brought from Africa and used as workers on the large farms, or **plantations**, in the American South. They were slaves because they belonged to the plantation owners.

For many years, slavery was also allowed in Canada. In the days of New France, many Black people and some Aboriginal peoples were held as slaves. But in 1834, slavery became illegal in Canada.

Slavery continued in the United States, so many Black people seeking their freedom escaped north into Canada. They followed an escape route called the **Underground Railroad**. It brought about 30 000 Black people to Canada in the years before the American Civil War ended slavery.

A Closer Look

Slavery and the American Civil War

The American Civil War lasted from 1861 to 1865. It began when the southern part of the United States broke away to form a separate country, called the Confederate States of America. The government in the North did not want to allow the country to break up. War was the result.

One of the great issues of the war was slavery. Slavery began very early in American history. The slaves were bought and traded in Africa, then sent to America by sailing ships. In America, they were sold at auction to the highest bidder. It was the law that if Black slaves tried to run away from their owners, anyone was allowed to kill them. More than 9 million Black people were brought to America as slaves.

People in the South wanted to preserve slavery because their economy depended on the work done by slaves. Many Northerners wanted to abolish it. This was a major cause of the Civil War.

Finally, the Northern states were victorious. The United States stayed together, and slavery became illegal. There was no more need for the Underground Railroad.

This painting shows Black slaves escaping from the United States into Canada in the 1850s. It is a scene of the Underground Railroad at work.

HOW TO... Study an Illustration

Illustrations are important sources of information. Photographs, drawings, maps, sketches, and paintings are all types of illustrations. They can tell us a great deal about what life was like when the illustration was made.

Here are some questions to ask yourself when you are looking at an illustration:

1. What is the most important message in this picture? (Hint: What catches your attention first?)

2. What other details do you notice?

3. How do the details help you understand more?

What is the purpose of events such as Caribana? Can you think of events in your community that recognize a particular cultural group?

Black People in Canada Today

Today there are many thousands of Black Canadians. Some of them trace the arrival of their ancestors back to the American Revolution or even earlier. Others have come more recently, from Africa or from the islands of the Caribbean. It is a varied community that now calls Canada home.

Black Canadians celebrate their achievements in many ways, including Black History Month every February. During this time, special attention is paid to the role of Black people in Canadian history. One of the largest community events in the country is Caribana [Kair-uh-BAN-uh], a festival of Caribbean culture. It is held each July in downtown Toronto.

The Pacific Rim

If you look at a map of Canada, you will see that British Columbia is located in the Pacific Ocean. Now find British Columbia on a map of the world. You will see that across the Pacific lie Japan, China, and other Asian countries.

If you think of the Pacific Ocean as a bowl, you can see that these countries lie around the rim of the bowl. For this reason, countries that border on the Pacific are called **Pacific Rim** countries.

The ocean provides a convenient "highway" for trade and travel between countries of the Pacific Rim. In the past, British Columbia has been the doorway to Canada for many immigrants from Asia.

Early Asian Immigration

The first people to arrive in British Columbia from Asian countries came to find jobs. Life in their own countries was difficult. Good land was scarce, and many lived in poverty. In British Columbia, they hoped to prosper.

The first Chinese came with the gold rush in 1858. They called British Columbia "Gold Mountain." Later, during the building of the railway across the continent in the 1880s, thousands of Chinese came to work as labourers on the line. Once the railway was built, they moved to the cities where they found jobs as servants, farmers, and storekeepers. Others found work in the salmon canneries and coal mines.

Many immigrants also came to British Columbia from Japan and India. The Japanese were particularly attracted to the salmon fishing industry. People from India found jobs in the sawmills.

Chinatowns

When Chinese people arrived in Canada, they naturally wanted to live among friends and family. At the same time, the government thought it was best if the newcomers did not mix with other groups. Laws were passed to keep the Chinese in their own neighbourhoods. The neighbourhood came to be called **Chinatown**.

Victoria had the first Chinatown in Canada, starting with the arrival of the Chinese in 1858. Later, the Chinatown in Vancouver became the largest in Canada. Many other communities in British Columbia also had Chinatowns.

The Chinese were not alone in creating their own neighbourhoods. Many immigrant groups preferred to live together in familiar surroundings. Larger cities had areas where immigrants from places like Italy, Poland, or South America lived. All the different groups mixed with each other in different ways—at school, at work, or in the streets. But they also had their own neighbourhoods where they could meet friends, buy special food items in the stores, and celebrate the customs of their cultures.

Today, these neighbourhoods are lively, interesting parts of our communities. We go there to shop, eat in the restaurants, or attend cultural festivals. They are good places to learn about the customs and traditions of other people.

Meeting with Prejudice

Even though Canada is a country built by immigrants, newcomers are sometimes made to feel unwelcome by other Canadians. This was the case for many years with newcomers from Asia.

Many non-Asians wanted to keep British Columbia British. They thought the Asian newcomers would not be able to fit in to Canadian society. They feared that the newcomers would take all the jobs.

Laws were passed to keep Asian peoples out of Canada. One way

was to charge a tax they could not afford. Starting in 1885, every Chinese coming to Canada had to pay $50. Later on this tax went as high as $500. It was called a "head tax" because it was charged per person.

Still, some Chinese could afford to pay the tax, so on 1 July 1923, the government passed a law banning Chinese immigration completely. Chinese Canadians remember that day as "Humiliation Day." Other laws were passed making it impossible for immigrants from Japan and India to vote or to hold certain jobs.

A Change of Mind

After many years, attitudes toward the Asian newcomers became more welcoming. Laws were changed so that people from Asia could enter Canada just like anyone else. In 1947, the ban on Chinese immigration was lifted. That same year, Asian Canadians were granted the vote. They finally had the same rights that belong to all Canadians.

People who trace their background to countries in Asia play an important role in today's society in British Columbia.

This photograph shows a group of Chinese railway builders. The work was hard and dangerous, and the wages were low. Chinese workers were forced to live apart in rundown shacks. Why do you think so many of them put up with these conditions?

REAL PEOPLE: DAVID LAM

David Lam brought his family to live in Vancouver in 1967. He was a successful banker in Hong Kong, but in Vancouver he began to buy and sell property. He became very wealthy. Along with his wife Dorothy, he set up a charity and gave a lot of his money away. The Lams have given money to universities, hospitals, and churches.

In 1988, David Lam became the **lieutenant-governor** [loo-TEN-unt GUV-ur-nur] of British Columbia. He was the first Canadian of Chinese background to hold such a position anywhere in Canada. He served as lieutenant-governor for seven years.

Mr. Lam once compared immigration to a dinner invitation. "Coming to Canada is like coming to a potluck dinner. If everyone brings leftovers, we'll have a leftover dinner. But if one spends some of one's time, picks one's best recipe, and is prepared to give one's best, we will have a feast."

In Chapter 2, you read about the queen's representative in Canada, the governor general. In each province, the queen is represented by a **lieutenant-governor**. Like the governor general, the duties of a lieutenant-governor are ceremonial.

Find Out

In the photo on this page, David Lam is wearing the uniform of the lieutenant-governor. Find out

- who appoints the lieutenant-governor

- what some of the duties of a lieutenant-governor are

Think For Yourself

Discuss with a partner what David Lam meant when he compared immigration to a "potluck dinner." Then share your ideas with the class.

The Hutterites

Over the years, Canada has welcomed many religious groups. There has never been an official religion in Canada. All religions are allowed and respected. In some countries, this is not the case. Sometimes groups that are being persecuted (treated badly) in their own countries for their beliefs choose to move to Canada.

One example of such a group is the Hutterites [HUT-ur-ites]. Hutterites are named after the founder of their religion, Jacob Hutter. Originally, they lived in eastern Europe. Hutterites believe in a simple, farming lifestyle. They are **pacifists** [PAS-ih-fists]—they try to live peacefully and refuse to take part in wars. They believe that most possessions belong to the group, not to individuals.

Hutterites live in farming colonies consisting of several families. As much as possible, they avoid contact with the wider world. The colonies have their own schools and forms of government.

Because of their beliefs, Hutterites were badly treated in Europe. They moved from country to country, looking for a home where they would be allowed to live in peace. In 1918, a large number came to Canada and settled mainly in the Prairie provinces.

Today in Canada there are about 20 000 Hutterites, who continue to lead the traditional Hutterite way of life.

Most Hutterite colonies support themselves through agriculture.

Think For Yourself

What does the term *religious freedom* mean to you? How are the Hutterites an example of religious freedom? Do you think the government ever has the right to tell people what religious ideas they should have? Why or why not? Think about whether religious freedom makes Canada a better place in which to live. Discuss your ideas with a partner, then share them with the class.

Find Out

In this chapter, you have read about different groups of immigrants who came to Canada in the past. These included people from China, Black people from the United States, and Hutterites from Europe. Many other groups of people have immigrated to Canada. For example, Doukhobors [DOOK-uh-borz] came to Canada from Russia, as did Mennonites and Ukrainians. More recently, many newcomers arrived from Iran, a country in the Middle East.

Do a research project on one of these groups. Here are five questions you can use to focus your investigation:

- *When did most of the people in this group come to Canada?*
- *Why did they come?*
- *Where in Canada did most of them settle?*
- *What are two or three traditions or ceremonies belonging to this group?*
- *What contributions have they made to Canadian society?*

Once you have collected your information, decide how you will present it. Use the five questions to organize your ideas under headings.

Looking Back

In this chapter, you saw that Canada is made up of people from many different places. You had a chance to think about the contributions they make to Canadian society. You also learned that newcomers sometimes have to struggle against prejudice.

Do you think it is important for Canada to welcome immigrants from other countries? Why or why not?

Chapter 4

Living Together

Think for a moment about the part each person plays in making your school a success. Your teachers lead the classes and organize the learning that goes in the school. The librarian helps you find the books you need. The custodians keep the school clean.

Do you have a role in making the school a success?

A country is something like a school. Every person who lives there has a role in making it an interesting and successful place. We are all different. Each of us has certain talents and backgrounds. Each of us has something unique to contribute to the community.

In this chapter, you can learn about the idea of citizenship. You'll discover how people of many talents, from many backgrounds, live and work together to create a successful country. You can begin to learn in class by discussing what qualities you think make a good citizen.

Working Together

Citizens are people who belong to a community. That community might be as small as your classroom or as large as your country. In both cases, the community is a group and you are a member.

Not everyone who belongs to a community is the same. Think about your class, as an example. Everyone in it is a very different person. But there is one thing you all share. You are all members of the class. That is your community.

As members of the class, you share something else. You share the *responsibility* to make the group a success. You don't have to agree with everything the group does. Disagreements are part of every community. What makes the community a success is being able to find ways to get along in spite of disagreements.

HOW TO... Work in a Group

Working in a group means sharing ideas and sharing tasks. Here are some suggestions for making group work successful:

1. Encourage every member of the group to take part in discussions. Don't worry about always getting the right answers. All ideas are useful.

2. Try not to talk too much! Leave time for everyone to contribute. If you exclude someone, you may be excluding some good ideas.

3. When there are a lot of jobs to be done, share them. Use everyone's talents.

4. Even if you disagree with someone, try to understand the other person's idea. You aren't the only person with good ideas. Perhaps there will be some part of the idea that you can agree with.

Try This

One thing that all groups do is welcome their new members. As a country, Canada welcomes newcomers who arrive from other countries to live here. As a class, you welcome new students who have come to join you.

Working in a small group, identify some reasons why a new student might feel unwelcome in your class. Identify things that can be done in each case to make the new student feel more at home. Organize the reasons and solutions in a chart like the one shown here.

Reasons	Solutions
1. newcomer doesn't know anyone in the class	1. appoint an official greeter to make the newcomer at home
2.	2.
3.	3.

In your group, make a poster that could be used to welcome new students.

When all the groups have completed their posters, share your ideas about working in groups with the rest of the class. What are the advantages? What are the disadvantages?

When working in a group, remember to speak up when you have an idea or opinion. Give reasons for what you think.

Citizenship

You began this chapter by discussing the qualities that make a good citizen. Has your experience working in groups helped you to think of other qualities? Now you can consider another question. What does it mean to be a citizen? What rights does a citizen have that a non-citizen doesn't have?

Citizens are people who have full membership in a community. They have all the rights and freedoms that allow them to participate fully in society. Citizens may vote in elections.

They can hold passports. They are allowed to run as candidates in elections. In order to work at some professions, a person must be a citizen. These are some of the advantages of **citizenship**.

But citizenship also brings responsibilities. Citizens are expected to play a role in making their society a success. In time of war, they are sometimes called on to defend their country. They are expected to obey the law, to take part in elections, and to treat other citizens with respect.

A group of new Canadians take the oath of citizenship. If you moved to another country, would you become a citizen there, or would you keep your Canadian citizenship?

I swear (or affirm)
that I will be faithful and bear
true allegiance to Her Majesty,
Queen Elizabeth the Second,
Queen of Canada, Her Heirs
and Successors, and that I will
faithfully observe the laws of Canada
and fulfill my duties as
a Canadian citizen.

Becoming Canadian

How does someone become a citizen? If you are born in Canada, you become a Canadian citizen automatically. New residents of Canada are welcome to become Canadians too, but first they must live in the country for three years. They must show that they speak either English or French. They must also have some knowledge of Canadian institutions (our laws, practices, and customs). For instance, they must understand the system of elections and how the government works.

When they are ready, newcomers appear before a judge and swear allegiance, or loyalty, to their new home. They are then granted Canadian citizenship.

This process of becoming Canadian is called **naturalization.** Whether they were born in Canada or were naturalized, all Canadians have the same rights under the law.

Before 1947, Canadians were not actually called *Canadians*. In the law, they were called *British subjects*. In 1947, Parliament passed the Canadian Citizenship Act. For the first time, people who lived in Canada were officially known as Canadians

A Closer Look

Becoming a Canadian Citizen

Here are the steps a person must follow to become a Canadian citizen.

1. First you must
   - be 18 years of age or older. (Younger people must have someone else apply for them.)
   - have lived in Canada for three out of the previous four years.
   - speak either French or English.
   - know basic information about Canada. (This information is included in a special booklet given to all applicants.)
   - pay a fee of $200.

2. You then apply at an office of Citizenship and Immigration Canada.

3. Officials there gather some basic information about all applicants. They make sure that every applicant is in Canada legally and has not been convicted of any crimes.

4. After several months, you will receive a "Notice to Appear." This asks you to come to an office to take your citizenship test. The test checks your knowledge of Canada and your understanding of what citizenship means.

5. If you pass the test, you are asked to come to a special citizenship ceremony to take the oath of citizenship. Then you receive a certificate.

You are now a citizen of Canada.

Rung Thi Nguyen took the oath of citizenship on her 105th birthday.

In Ottawa, and across the country, Canada Day celebrations include a dazzling display of fireworks.

Try This

Here are some questions from the citizenship test. Can you answer them? If you don't know the answers, think of where you could go to gather the information. One good source is an encyclopedia of Canada. Your school library may have this type of reference book.

- *What is the capital city of Canada? What is the capital city of your province?*

- *How many provinces and territories are there in Canada?*

- *Canada has two official languages. What are they?*

- *What day of the year is Canada Day?*

- *How old must you be to vote in a national election?*

  Why do you think it is important for would-be citizens to know this information? Is there other information that you think is important for them to know?

What Is a Hero?

Some citizens make special contributions to their communities. They are called heroes because they have accomplished something important. Usually, their accomplishments benefit the whole community. When Terry Fox made his run across Canada, he was doing it to raise money to fight cancer. Everyone admired his courage.

Who would you consider to be your heroes: a sports star; a scientist who made a great discovery; an astronaut who flew to the moon; or a soldier who won a medal for bravery in the war? These are all examples of heroes.

We honour heroes for their bravery or their special deeds. Heroes show the best that is in all of us. They also play an important role in their communities.

Terry Fox attempted to run across Canada in 1980. After he ran 5373 kilometres, cancer spread to his lungs, and he was forced to stop. Terry raised millions of dollars for cancer research. Every year a fundraising run in his name brings in more money. Terry Fox made a difference in the lives of all Canadians.

Try This

Why not build a hero sandwich? Draw the outline of a sandwich. Find words in magazines or newspapers that you think describe a hero. Cut out the words and paste them into your drawing.

What qualities do you think a hero must possess?

Everyone Has Heroes

Heroes come from all backgrounds and from every community. They might be celebrities, but they are just as likely to be someone living next door. Not all heroes are famous. Terry Fox was just a young student when he decided to make his run. Everyone is capable of being a hero.

REAL PEOPLE: ROBERTA, TOMMY, BIRUTÉ

ROBERTA BONDAR: ASTRONAUT

Roberta Bondar was the first Canadian woman to go into space.

She grew up in Sault Ste. Marie, Ontario. As a young woman, she learned to fly a plane and studied to become a doctor. In 1983, she was one of 4300 people who applied to be the first Canadians to go into space with the United States space program. Six lucky people were chosen. Dr. Bondar was the only woman.

She made her flight into space for eight days in January 1992, aboard the space shuttle *Discovery*. While the shuttle orbited around the earth, she conducted experiments that will help astronauts live more comfortably in space in the future.

Roberta Bondar is now a university professor in Ontario.

TOMMY PRINCE: WAR HERO

When Tommy Prince was a youngster growing up on a First Nations reserve north of Winnipeg, he spent a lot of time hunting and trapping. As a result, he became a crack shot with a rifle.

When the Second World War began, he joined the army, along with many other Aboriginal peoples. Because of his keen eyesight and tracking skills, he became a sniper (an expert shot who fires on the enemy from a hiding place). He was placed with a special team of **paratroopers**—soldiers who parachute into action from planes. Prince fought in Italy and France, winning many medals for bravery.

After the war he returned to Manitoba. When fighting broke out in Korea in 1950, he joined up again. Once more he stood out for his bravery in action.

In total, Tommy Prince was awarded ten medals for bravery, more than any other Aboriginal soldier.

BIRUTÉ GALDIKAS: SCIENTIST

Biruté Galdikas [beer-OO-tay GAL-dee-kus] came to live in Canada when she was just a baby. Her parents were from Lithuania, a small country in northern Europe. The Second World War had destroyed their homeland. They were looking for a place to make a fresh start.

Galdikas studied anthropology at university and became an expert on the orangutan, one of the great apes. Orangutans live in Borneo, an island in the South Pacific.

In 1971, Galdikas went to live in the jungles of Borneo. Her home was a small hut. Every day she followed the orangutans as they went about their lives in the wild. She became extremely close to these fascinating creatures.

Biruté Galdikas still lives part of every year in Borneo, where she works to protect the orangutans from hunters and other threats. The rest of the year she teaches in British Columbia at Simon Fraser University.

Try This

Let's see if you recognize the names of some Canadian heroes. Listed below are the names of seven people who have made special accomplishments. Try to match the names on the left to the descriptions on the right. You may know some of the names from the news or from your previous studies. Use the resources in the library to find out about the people whose names you do not recognize.

- Craig Kielburger

- Rick Hansen

- Nellie McClung

- John A. MacDonald

- Wayne Gretzky

- Ethel Blondin Andrew

- Justine Blainey

- fought in the courts for the right to play hockey on a boy's team

- first Aboriginal woman elected to Parliament

- began, at age 12, to campaign against the use of child labour around the world

- one of the greatest hockey players of all time

- drove his wheelchair around the world to raise money for medical research

- helped to win the vote for women

- Canada's first prime minister

Think For Yourself

Imagine that you have been put in charge of finding a way to honour each of the heroes listed on page 58. Try to come up with an idea for each person. Perhaps you could name a street or school after them or put up a statue. You'll have many ideas of your own. Share them with the rest of the class.

Wayne Gretzky was inducted (admitted) into the Hockey Hall of Fame in November 1999.

Try This

Advertise for a hero. Design a "Heroes Wanted" advertisement for television or a magazine. What would the job description be? What qualities would you ask for? What type of experience would be necessary?

Multiculturalism

Reading Hint

If you come to a word you don't know, try to figure it out. When you come to the word again, think about the beginning sound and what word might make sense.

*I*n Canada today, you often hear the word **multiculturalism**. What do you think the word means?

The next time you take a drive through your town or city, pay close attention to your surroundings. Here are some of the things you might see:

- a van delivering pizza

- people playing a game of cricket in the park

- a totem pole standing outside a public building

- a Sikh temple with its ornate roof

All of these things can be seen in most Canadian communities. Each of them represents one of many different cultures. That is why we say that Canada is *multicultural*. Pizza is a food that comes from Italy. Cricket is a game first played by the British. Totem poles are giant carvings made by First Nations people. Sikh temples are places of religious worship used by some South Asian people.

But no matter where they come from, we now recognize these things to be part of Canadian life.

One Society, Many Cultures

In the last chapter, you read about immigrants from many countries coming to Canada to start new lives. In the process, they created a new kind of society. The new society combined Aboriginal peoples and people of many different cultures from all over the world. This is what we mean when we say that Canada is a multicultural society.

It is only since the 1970s that Canadians have become used to calling their society multicultural. In 1971, the government of Prime Minister Pierre Trudeau [troo-DOH] made multiculturalism official government policy. Before that time, Canadians considered their country to be **bicultural**. The majority of people were either French or British in background.

Multiculturalism was a new way of looking at Canadian

society. It said that there are many cultures in Canada, and each one makes an important contribution to the country.

Multiculturalism has three main ideas:

- The federal government recognizes that Canadian society is made up of people of many different cultural backgrounds.

- The government helps people and organizations that are trying to protect and promote cultural heritages. These include dance groups, writers, community festivals, and so on.

- Through its policies and programs, the government encourages respect and equality for all Canadians, no matter where they came from originally.

Is this what you thought multiculturalism meant? Has your understanding of the word changed?

Almost any city street in Canada shows the many cultures that make up our country. What cultural backgrounds do you see evidence of in this scene?

Try This

Make a collage that shows diversity in Canada. Cut images out of magazines and newspapers that reflect several different cultures. These images can be faces, street signs, advertisements, or businesses. They can be images of almost anything. Paste the images on a large sheet of paper.

When you have finished, explain to the rest of the class how each image represents a different cultural background. Be sure to include your own cultural heritage in the collage!

A Closer Look

Place Names

The names of communities reflect the many cultures in Canada. Place names come from many sources. Vancouver is named for a famous British explorer, Captain George Vancouver, who arrived at the future site of the city in 1792. Gimli, a community in Manitoba, was founded by a group of immigrants from Iceland. Gimli means "paradise" in the Icelandic language. Sault Ste. Marie [soo saynt mah-REE], a city in Ontario, is located at the rapids in a river. Sault is a French word meaning "rapids" or "falls," and *Sainte-Marie* is a saint in the Roman Catholic religion. The place was named many years ago by Jesuit missionaries from Quebec.

In 1987, Frobisher Bay became officially known as Iqaluit. The name, which means "place of fish" in Inuktitut, has been used by Inuit for a long time.

Find Out

Where did the name of your own community come from? Does it reflect one of Canada's many cultures? Brainstorm in class to see what ideas you have about place names. For example, Fort Langley may have been named during the fur trade. Thompson and Baxter were probably named after people.

Choose five other place names of communities across Canada. Do some research to find out how the places got their names. Encyclopedias usually contain this information. The library also has many books of place names. If the place is nearby, you could telephone the community hall or museum, and ask for this information.

What do the names reveal about the history of each community?

Try This

Imagine that you have been asked to rename your community. Or perhaps you have been asked to name a street or a school. What name would you choose?

You could create **heritage markers**. These are signs that are erected in a public place explaining how a community got its name and the importance of that name. What does the name you chose reveal about the place you named?

~ LORD BYNG HIGH SCHOOL ~

This school was named after Viscount Byng of Vimy.
He was a British cavalry officer who was put in charge
of Canadian soldiers in the First World War. After
the war, he was governor general of Canada from
1921 to 1926. Lord Byng lived from 1862 to 1935.

Looking Back

In this chapter, you explored the meaning of citizenship. You saw that every community has heroes who reflect the best of that community. You also learned that Canada is a multicultural society.

Why is it important for people to take an active role in their communities?

Chapter 5

Government and the Constitution

Government is the way a group of people come together to organize their affairs.

Imagine for a moment that the government stopped working. What impact would this have on your life? Think about how many times during the day you use public, or government, services.

For example, your school was built and is operated by the government. When you go home today, there may be a letter waiting for you. The postal carrier who delivered it works for the government. When your soccer team plays a game during the weekend, it will be using a field looked after by the local parks board. The parks board is part of the government. Can you suggest other examples?

Government plays a major role in all our lives. In this chapter, you can learn how government in Canada is organized. But first of all, let's take a trip to Ottawa, the centre of government in Canada.

Welcome to Ottawa!

Ottawa is the capital city of Canada. It is a place where government is the main activity. Ottawa has many buildings that are used by the government to carry on the country's business.

The Parliament Buildings are located in the middle of downtown Ottawa. They have been the home of Canada's government since 1866. This is where the **politicians** meet to debate laws and make decisions. The Centre Block of the Parliament Buildings burned down in 1916, but it was rebuilt. If you go to Ottawa, you can take a tour of the Parliament Buildings.

Actually, that sounds like a good idea. Let's go to Ottawa and take a tour of Canada's capital city.

Politicians are people who are elected to form the government and make laws.

The Parliament Buildings in Ottawa are one of Canada's most popular tourist attractions. The tall central tower is called the Peace Tower. It contains a carillon, which is a set of huge bells that are played like a piano at a giant keyboard. When the carillon is playing, the bells can be heard all across the city.

The route of our tour. The boldface numbers in the text on pages 66 to 68 correspond to the numbers on this map.

A Bus Tour Of Ottawa

All aboard! Our bus is leaving for a tour of downtown Ottawa. There is a lot to see and we don't want to miss anything.

The tour starts on Wellington Street in front of the Supreme Court Building **(1)**. The Supreme Court is the most powerful court in Canada. It consists of nine judges who decide on only the most important cases. As the highest court in the country, the Supreme Court's decisions are final. They cannot be **appealed**.

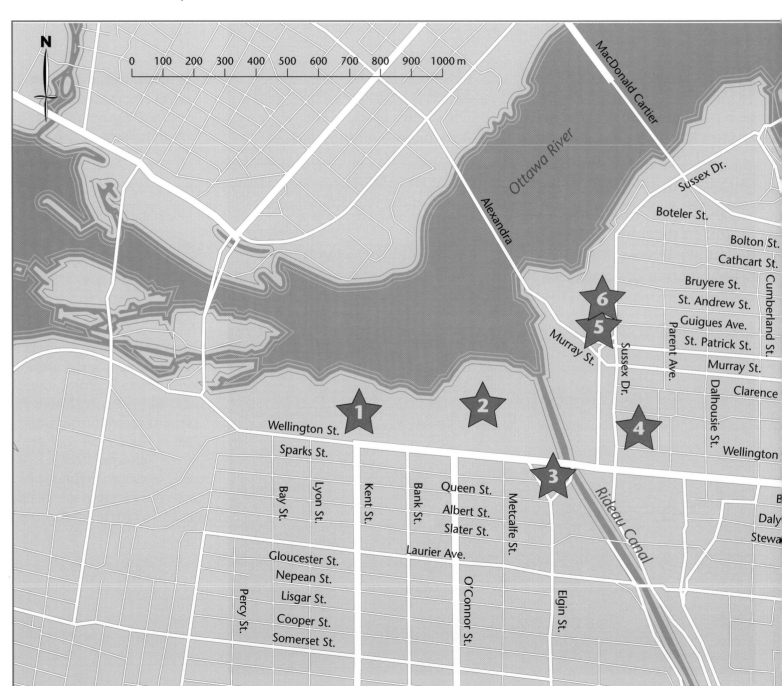

Continuing up Wellington Street, the bus arrives outside the Parliament Buildings **(2)**. The centre building, with the Peace Tower, is called the Centre Block. It contains the House of Commons, where all the laws are passed. The prime minister's office is in the Centre Block. The building on the right is called the East Block, and the building on the left is called the West Block. Both of these buildings contain government offices.

Do you notice the fountain in the middle of the open square? It seems to be on fire. It has an "eternal flame," which is fed by gas and never goes out.

After the bus passes the Parliament Buildings, be sure to look to your right. The open area is called Confederation Square **(3)**, and in the middle is a giant sculpture. It is the National War Memorial, erected in 1939 as a tribute to Canadian soldiers killed in the wars.

As our bus turns the corner onto Sussex Drive, we begin driving along the "mile of history." This is a stretch running down Sussex Drive to Government House, the home of the governor general. It is called the "mile of history" because there are so many old, historic buildings.

As we drive along Sussex Drive, look off to the right. You'll see a busy outdoor shopping area filled with fresh fruit and vegetable stalls. This is the Byward Market **(4)** where farmers have been selling their produce for 150 years.

Every year on November 11th, a crowd gathers at the National War Memorial to lay wreaths in memory of Canada's soldiers. At 11 a.m. there is a minute of silence. This marks the precise moment that the First World War ended on 11 November 1918.

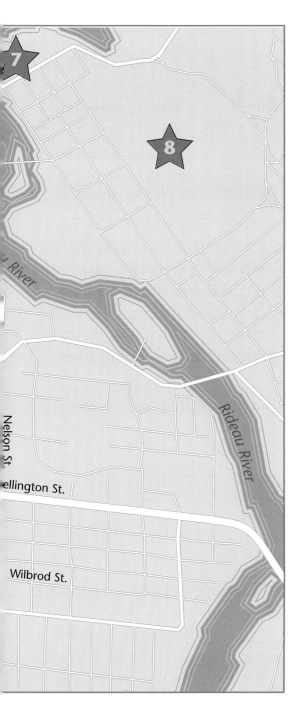

The Rideau Canal was opened in 1832. It extends from Ottawa all the way to Lake Ontario, 200 kilometres to the south. Part of it runs through the middle of Ottawa. In the winter, the canal is kept open as the longest outdoor skating rink in the world.

Ottawa was the centre of the logging industry when it started in the 1850s. We are driving through Lower Town, the old part of the city where the loggers and their families used to live.

Up ahead we can see the National Gallery of Canada on our left **(5)**. Let's stop for an hour and pay a visit. The gallery has a large collection of paintings by Canada's finest artists, as well as many paintings from other countries.

Back on the bus now, the tour continues down Sussex Drive, passing the Canadian War Museum **(6)** with the large tank outside. On our left, we can look across the Ottawa River and see the province of Quebec and the city of Hull. Perhaps on another visit, you'll have time to stop at the many interesting places on that side of the river.

We'll pause for a moment outside 24 Sussex Drive, one of Canada's most famous addresses **(7)**. It's the home of the prime minister. Since 1950, every prime minister has lived here.

Just down the street is a small gatehouse set at the entrance to a long driveway. We've arrived at Government House, also known as Rideau Hall, home of the governor general **(8)**. It is actually a large estate, big enough to contain a cricket pitch, a curling rink, and an extensive garden.

Government House marks the end of our bus tour. But there is still a little time left in the day. Let's strap on our skates and go for a spin on the canal!

A Closer Look

Ottawa

Here are some interesting facts about the city:

- Ottawa has been the capital of Canada since 1858.

- The Rideau Canal runs through the middle of Ottawa. In the winter, the water in the canal freezes and turns into a giant skating rink. People can skate to their jobs!

- Ottawa is located where the Rideau River, the Ottawa River, and the Gatineau River all come together. The Ottawa River forms the border between Ontario and Quebec. Ottawa is in Ontario, but right across the river is Quebec. As a result, many people who live in Ottawa speak both French and English.

- The name *Ottawa* is also the name of the local First Nations people. In their language, *Ottawa* (or *Odawa*) means "traders." So a translation of the name might be "place of the traders" or "the place where trading takes place." Where does the name of your community come from?

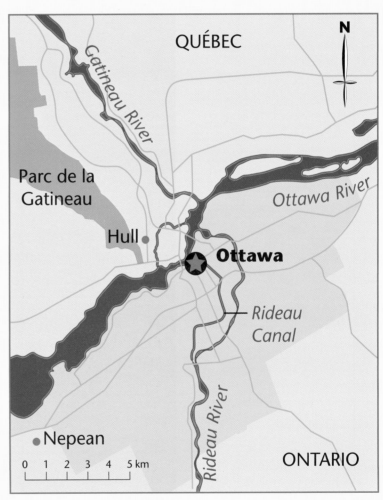

Ottawa is located where three rivers meet. Why do you think this was considered a good place to start a community?

Think For Yourself

There are probably many interesting places in your community that visitors might like to see. How would you help them learn about your community? A bus tour is one way, but there are others. For example, a short walking tour could be just as interesting.

Step one. Look around your community. Decide on the neighbourhood where you want to have a walking tour.

Step two. Make a list of six or seven interesting places on the tour. Perhaps you could call them "stops of interest." You might have to do some research to collect information about these places. What are your reasons for choosing each stop of interest? For example, was it associated with a famous person? Is it very old?

Old houses often have fascinating stories to tell.

Step three. Make a sketch map of the neighbourhood. Put numbers on the map to show where your stops of interest are located.

Step four. Write a brief paragraph about each stop of interest, using the information you gathered. For example: *The Brixton House. This old home, built in 1873, was owned by the first settler in the area. It is believed to be haunted by the ghost of his young daughter, who died of smallpox when she was 13 years old.*

Step five. Put the written information together with the sketch map. You now have a small guide book, perfect for guiding people around your tour.

It's time to lead your first tour!

How Government Works

Ottawa is the capital of Canada. It is the headquarters of the federal (national) government. It is where decisions are made that affect all Canadians. The federal government meets in the Parliament Buildings, which you visited on your bus tour.

The purpose of government is to make laws. Laws are the rules by which society operates. Every society or group needs to have rules so that members can live securely and know what is expected of them.

Your school probably has a student government. It has the job of running some of the events in the school. On a small scale, your student government is similar to the different levels of government in the country.

Try This

As a class, brainstorm a list of things that your student government does. Then suggest other things that you think it could be doing. Decide on a way to present your suggestions to the members of the student government.

After your brainstorming, complete this sentence: *We need student government because . . .*

Levels of Government

You have already learned something about the federal government. This is the national level of government. There are two other levels of government in Canada. Remember that your student government took responsibility for certain things around the school. Similarly, each level of government in the country takes responsibility for different issues.

- Provincial government is the government in your province. It looks after matters of concern to everyone in the province. The provincial government meets in the **legislature** of each province.

- Local government is the government in your community. It looks after issues of concern to the local community. Local government usually meets as a town or city **council**.

Each level of government has responsibility for the things that it can do best. For example, the federal government is in charge of organizing the armed forces. It is not necessary for every province (or every community!) to have its own army. There is one armed forces to protect all Canadians.

On the other hand, local government is in charge of fixing your sidewalks and streets. You would not expect people in faraway Ottawa to know about potholes and flooded drains in every street in the country. These are matters best left to the government that is closest to the community.

Sometimes there are problems that are so big they require more than one level of government to handle them. In these cases, two governments will often share the responsibility.

Think For Yourself

Here is a list of five responsibilities that the government has. Which level of government do you think is responsible in each case? Ask yourselves: *Which level of government is closest to the issue?*

- university education
- drinking water
- protection of wildlife that is in danger of disappearing
- immigration
- drivers' licences

When you have decided, do some research to find out if you are correct.

The Federal Government

The men and women who are elected to the federal government are called **Members of Parliament** (**MPs**). They are chosen in national elections that must take place at least every five years. There are 295 MPs, though the number goes up as the population of Canada grows. The country is divided into 295 districts, called **ridings**, and each riding elects its own MP.

Members of Parliament hold their meetings in the Parliament Buildings in Ottawa in a large chamber known as the House of Commons. Visitors are welcome. You can sit in the Visitors' Gallery and listen to MPs discussing government business.

Parliament actually has two levels, or "houses." The House of Commons is one level. The other House of Parliament is called the **Senate**, sometimes known as the Upper House. Unlike Members of Parliament, members of the Senate, called **senators**, are not elected. They are appointed to their positions by the government. The 104 senators have their own meeting room, called the Senate Chamber.

The purpose of the Senate is to approve all laws that have been passed by the House of Commons. The job of the senators is to examine these laws to make sure that they are in the best interests of the country.

Senators may remain in office until they are 75 years old. Then they must retire. Senators are usually prominent people from all walks of life.

Senators meet in the Senate Chamber to pass laws and to listen to the concerns of groups and individuals affected by a law. There is also a Question Period when senators may inquire about government actions and policies.

Abolish [uh-BOL-ish] means to put an end to a law or custom.

Think For Yourself

Some people think that the Senate is undemocratic. They feel this way because senators are not elected—they cannot claim to speak for anyone but themselves. Why should they be able to influence what the elected Members of Parliament decide? Others think the Senate should be **abolished** because it is unnecessary.

On the other hand, some people think the Senate serves an important role. They argue that because it is not elected, the Senate is not as easily pressured by public opinion.

Use a chart like the one shown here to organize both points of view on the issue.

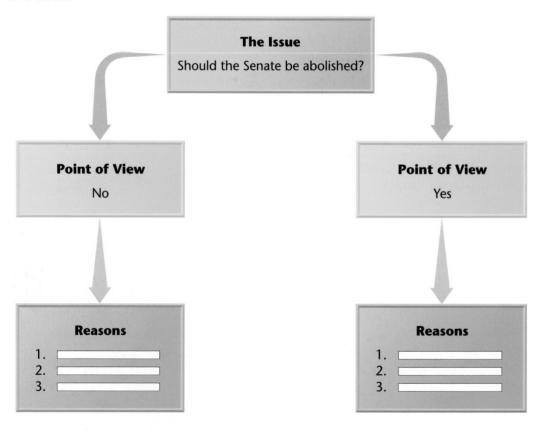

The Issue

Should the Senate be abolished?

Point of View

No

Point of View

Yes

Reasons

1.
2.
3.

Reasons

1.
2.
3.

What do you think? Discuss the issue in small groups. Analyze the different points of view, then form your own opinion.

The Provincial Government

Every province has its own government. Members are elected from around the province and carry out their duties in the capital city of the province. Just as Ottawa has Parliament, so each province has its own legislature. In British Columbia, the legislative assembly is in Victoria. The people elected to the provincial government are called **Members of the Legislative Assembly (MLAs)**.

Provincial governments have only one "house." There are no Senates in the provinces, only the elected assembly.

Each province is divided into many electoral districts, or ridings, and each riding elects an MLA. Each riding has approximately the same population. The MLA represents his or her riding in the legislative assembly.

Your Local Government

Local governments manage the affairs of the local community. Every city, town, and village has its own government. A typical local government provides services such as

- fire protection
- public libraries
- public transportation (bus, subway)
- snow removal

The usual form of local government consists of a mayor and an elected council. The mayor is the chief officer. He or she leads the meetings of council and represents the community at official events.

Sometimes several communities located close to one another get together to provide services in common. In this way, the cost of services for each community decreases. This is known as regional government.

In a federal or provincial election, voters make their choice on a piece of paper called a ballot. The ballot is then folded and put into a locked box.

A Closer Look

Voting

Democracy [dih-MOK-ruh-see] is a form of self-government. Its basic principle (belief) is that people rule themselves. We are not told by someone else what to do. We make the decisions ourselves.

Of course, we can't all be involved in government all the time. We have other jobs to do. So we choose people to represent us in government. This is still a form of self-government because we are choosing our own leaders to make decisions on our behalf. If we don't like what the government is doing, we can always choose a new one at the next election.

The vote, then, is the basic tool of self-government. We use it to choose the people who will represent us in government. But not everyone is allowed to vote. Young people do not have the vote. You have to be at least 18 years old to vote in an election. You also have to be a Canadian citizen. In a provincial election, you have to be a resident of the province.

Over the years, people have been denied a vote for many reasons.

- Women were not allowed to vote in national elections until 1918. Government was considered "man's work." It took many years of effort by women to gain their basic democratic right.

- Naturalized Canadians from China, Japan, and India didn't get the vote until 1948.

- Inuit weren't allowed to vote until 1950, and First Nations didn't get the vote until 1960.

Gradually, all adult Canadians have received the same right to vote in elections, but it has been a long process.

Nellie McClung fought to gain the provincial vote for women in Manitoba and Alberta.

HOW TO... Influence Government

Taking part in elections is one way that people choose the kind of government they have. But elections happen only once every few years. Does this mean that you can influence the government only at election time?

Not at all. People try in many ways to have a say in how the government is managing affairs—whether or not it is election time.

If you feel strongly about an issue in your community, the country, or even in the world, here are some ways to influence the government:

1. Write a letter to your MP, your MLA, or your member of local council. Express your opinion and suggest what you think should be done. Remember always to ask for an answer. Keep track of the issue to see whether any change takes place.

2. Start a petition asking the government to take some action. Collect signatures from your friends and people in the neighbourhood. Then send off the petition. All these signatures will show the government that many people care about the issue.

3. Local government is usually the easiest to approach. It meets right in your community, and the meetings are open to the public. Find out where the council meetings take place and attend one of them. Make your views known.

Try This

In class, brainstorm other ways that you can influence government.

Be aware that any issue involves different points of view. Try to learn about all points of view before making up your own mind.

Craig Kielburger (*back row, middle*), a young Canadian, started Free the Children when he was 12 years old. The organization campaigns against child labour and promotes children's rights throughout the world.

Think For Yourself

Is there an issue that you care about? It could be anything from paving the sidewalk on your street to providing more money for children in another country so that they will have enough to eat. Choose one of the actions described on page 77, and *use your influence to make change happen.*

Set specific goals for your action. For example, if you decide to collect signatures on a petition, decide how many signatures you want to have. You will also have to think about ways of deciding whether or not your action had any results.

Making Rules for Working Together

Imagine for a moment that you want to form a club. It could be any sort of club—a hiking club or a cleanup club to keep your school grounds free of garbage.

First, find some friends to join the club. Then come up with some rules so that members will know what they are expected to do and when they are expected to do it. This set of rules is called the club's **constitution** [kon-stuh-TOO-shun].

Just like your club, countries have constitutions as well. A constitution is a document that sets down the basic rules of government.

Canada's Constitution

In Canada, the Constitution states what powers belong to the government. It also declares that all Canadians have certain rights.

The Charter of Rights and Freedoms

When Canada created its new Constitution in 1982, it included a new document, the Charter of Rights and Freedoms. The Charter declares that every Canadian has the same rights, and it lists these rights. No one is allowed to violate these rights, not even the government. They are guaranteed by the Charter.

Every Canadian has these basic rights:

- the right to vote in elections

- the right to follow any religion

- the right to belong to any organization

- the right to move freely from place to place in Canada

- the right not to be put in prison for no reason

- the right to a fair trial if accused of a crime

For many years, the Canadian Constitution was the British North America Act, passed by the British Parliament in 1867. It gave Canada most of the powers of an independent country, but not all of them. For instance, Canada did not have the power to change its own Constitution. In 1982, Canada created a new Constitution Act that gave the country full independence.

These are only a few. The Charter of Rights and Freedoms guarantees many other rights to all Canadians.

One section of the Charter of Rights and Freedoms (Section 15) promises **equality** to all Canadians. What does *equality* mean? Does it mean that everyone has the same talents and abilities? Does it mean that everyone should be treated the same under the law?

Unhappily, Canadians do not always treat each other equally. Sometimes people show prejudice toward someone from a different country or different background. You have already read about the poor treatment received by some people who immigrated to Canada. This is an example of prejudice.

This is Section 15(1) of the Charter of Rights and Freedoms.

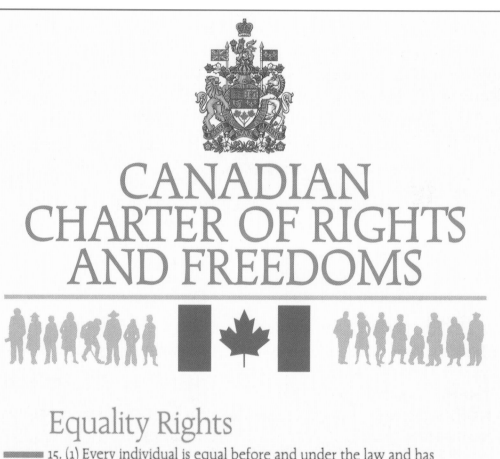

CANADIAN CHARTER OF RIGHTS AND FREEDOMS

Equality Rights

15. (1) Every individual is equal before and under the law and has the right to the equal protection and equal benefit of the law without discrimination and, in particular, without discrimination based on race, national or ethnic origin, colour, religion, sex, age or mental or physical disability. (2) Subsection (1) does not preclude any law, program or activity that has as its object the amelioration of conditions of disadvantaged individuals or groups including those that are disadvantaged because of race, national or ethnic origin, colour, religion, sex, age or mental or physical disability.

Try This

Is everyone in your school treated equally? Does everyone get the same use of the facilities?

In small groups, look for ways you think your school could be made a more equal place. Share your findings with the rest of the class. After you've discussed all the groups' findings, make a list of two or three of the most important ones. Decide on what improvements would make the school a more equal place.

Think For Yourself

Now it's time to take action. Decide on the best way to present your suggested improvements to the principal. Perhaps you should write a letter. Or you could organize a group of students to meet with the principal. It's your decision!

Looking Back

In this chapter, you learned about government and the way it is organized. You also discovered the importance of a constitution.

Do you think it is important for everyone to take an interest in what the government is doing? Why or why not?

Chapter 6

Aboriginal Peoples and Government

*Y*ou have learned that there are many different Aboriginal groups in Canada. Each group has its own customs and traditions. Many have their own languages, beliefs, and ways of living.

You have also seen that the Aboriginal peoples were the original inhabitants of Canada. They were here before the first European settlers arrived. For this reason, they have a special relationship with the government.

In this chapter, you can learn about this relationship between the government and Aboriginal peoples in Canada.

Aboriginal Government

*I*n the last chapter, you learned that government is the way a group of people organizes its affairs. All groups have some sort of government.

Aboriginal peoples had systems of government. These systems varied from group to group, but they shared many things in common.

Living in Groups

The Aboriginal peoples lived together in family groups. Members worked together to gather food and to build their homes. At certain times of the year, the groups met to socialize and take part in special ceremonies.

Most groups had some type of leader. Sometimes this was a chief who inherited the position. In other cases, leaders gained influence because they were admired for their bravery or their wisdom. For example, a leader might be a better hunter or a braver warrior than anyone else. When a leader lost the respect of the people, he or she would lose influence and no longer be looked on as a leader.

Many Aboriginal peoples lived together in small family groups. Do you think it would be easier for family groups to reach agreement than for all the members of your community? Why or why not?

Aboriginal peoples have particular respect for their Elders. They believe that life experience has given the Elders special wisdom. Elders help the children to learn about traditional knowledge and history. They also take part in community decision making. Can you suggest reasons why Elders might have special knowledge to share? What role do Elders play in your family? in your community?

Making Decisions

Aboriginal peoples did not use voting in their system of government. They had a form of government that was different from the European way. There were no elections and no parliaments.

Instead, most Aboriginal groups made decisions by **consensus** [kun-SEN-sus]. Everyone who wanted to could express an opinion. An issue was discussed until everyone in the group agreed on what to do.

By contrast, a system of voting works by majority rule. The person or choice that earns the most votes wins. This is the decision of the majority of people. Those people who voted against the winning choice go along with the decision anyway because they accept the system of majority rule.

A Different Way

When Europeans came to Canada, they did not understand the Aboriginal way of government. Aboriginal societies did not have any written laws. It was hard to see how they chose their leaders. Europeans thought the Aboriginal peoples had no government because the system was so different from their own.

Europeans thought their way of doing things was best. They ignored the wishes of the Aboriginal peoples and established their own form of government in Canada.

Try This

Write out your own definition of *majority* and *consensus*. Compare your understanding with the definitions from the rest of the class.

Make a list of words that have been used to describe *consensus* and *majority*. Which words are positive? Which are negative?

Aboriginal peoples were not allowed to take part in this new government. They did not have a vote, and they were not allowed to hold any government positions.

The new government negotiated **treaties** with some groups of Aboriginal peoples. These treaties were written agreements between the Aboriginal groups and the government. On the one side, Aboriginal peoples agreed to give up their traditional lands. On the other side, the government agreed to

- make cash payments to the Aboriginal groups

- set aside small areas of land, called **reserves**, for the use of First Nations groups

- permit the Aboriginal peoples to hunt and fish as they had always done

A Special Relationship

There is a special relationship between the government in Canada and the Aboriginal peoples. Treaties are a part of this relationship.

Because they were the first inhabitants of the land, Aboriginal peoples have special rights. In other words, they have these rights because they were here first. These are called **Aboriginal rights**, and they belong to Aboriginal peoples as a group. Aboriginal rights are part of the Canadian Constitution.

A series of 11 treaties was made in Canada between 1871 and 1921. These treaties covered much of Western Canada and the North. Before that, other treaties had been signed in Eastern Canada. Many parts of the country are still not covered by treaties. Only a small part of British Columbia, for example, has treaties.

After many years of inaction, treaties are again being made. In 1975, Cree people in northern Quebec signed an agreement that allowed much of their hunting lands to be flooded by a new power dam. In 1999, the Nisga'a people in northern British Columbia signed a treaty. That same year, the new territory of Nunavut was created in northern Canada. In Nunavut, the Inuit have a strong say in the way government operates.

Treaty making is an ongoing process. Treaties recognize that Aboriginal peoples have rights to their land.

Do you remember when the Inuit and First Nations were first allowed to vote in elections in Canada? If not, you can go back to Chapter 5 to find this information.

A Closer Look

Traditions

Traditions are important in any society. The old ways bring strength and meaning. Think of some of your own traditions. Traditions are important to Aboriginal peoples as well.

The Nuu-chah-nulth are First Nations people living on the west coast of Vancouver Island in British Columbia. One of the traditions of the Nuu-chah-nulth was hunting whales. Huge grey whales swim along the coast each year. Nuu-chah-nulth hunters used to go out in their canoes to chase them.

Only high-ranking chiefs were allowed to hunt the whales. They prepared themselves by participating in many ceremonies and prayers. While the whalers were hunting, their wives continued to follow certain rituals.

When a whale was harpooned and towed back to shore, the meat was shared with the entire village. A great feast was held in celebration.

The Nuu-chah-nulth did not kill many whales each season. Their hunt did not have an impact on the whale population. However, in the 1860s, American whalers began killing the grey whales in such huge numbers that they almost disappeared. During the 1930s, all whaling stopped. Now the whales have returned.

The Nuu-chah-nulth have announced that they want to go back to whaling. They say it is part of their traditions. Many people fear for the future of the whales. They are opposed to starting the hunt again.

Think For Yourself

Discuss the issue of whaling in class. Here are some things to think about:

- Whaling was an important part of Nuu-chah-nulth culture.

- The Nuu-chah-nulth have not hunted whales for many years.

- The grey whales were almost extinct because of hunting.

- There are as many grey whales today as there ever were.

- The Nuu-chah-nulth will only kill a few whales.

- People worry that if the Nuu-chah-nulth start hunting, so will other groups.

- Many tourists come to see the whales.

 Sort these ideas into two lists. Which of the ideas support whaling (pros)? Which argue against it (cons)? List your ideas in a pro/con chart like the one above.

Issue: Whaling	
Pros	Cons
1.	1.
2.	2.
3.	3.

The entire community celebrated a successful whale hunt. The meat from the whale was shared among everyone.

Whale-watching gives people the chance to observe whales in their natural setting.

Find Out

If possible, invite a Nuu-chah-nulth person to come to your class to present the Nuu-chah-nulth point of view about the whale hunt. You could also invite someone from an environmental group, such as Greenpeace, who is against the hunt. Think of five questions about the hunt to ask your visitors.

After you've considered both points of view, make up your own mind. Should whaling occur? Express your point of view in a poster that says clearly in words and pictures what you think about the whale hunt.

When Cultures Meet

When you meet people from another culture, there may be things you do not understand about the way they live. They may wear different clothes, eat different foods, or celebrate different holidays.

In Canada, we try to understand their ways, just as they try to understand ours. You have learned that Canada is a multicultural country. This means that Canadians accept differences. We believe that all people should have the right to honour their own traditions, as long as they do not harm anyone else.

Forcing Change

When the first Europeans to come to Canada met the Aboriginal peoples, they did not attempt to understand them. Instead, they tried to change them. The newcomers tried to force their own ways on the Aboriginal peoples.

Aboriginal peoples were willing to accept many of the new ways and to share useful skills with the newcomers. But they saw no reason why they should give up their own cultures. They wanted to keep their languages and their own way of life.

Soon the new settlers outnumbered the Aboriginal peoples. They wanted them to adopt the European religions and to live in communities where they would clear the land and begin farming—just like the European newcomers.

Through their government, the new settlers tried to force the Aboriginal peoples to change, to become more like Europeans. This policy was called **assimilation.**

The Indian Act

In 1876 the government of Canada passed into law the Indian Act. (It was called the Indian Act because, at the time,

Aboriginal peoples were called Indians.) This act outlined what Aboriginal peoples could and could not do. It brought almost every part of their lives under the control of the government. Under the act, Aboriginal peoples did not have the same rights as other Canadians.

The Indian Act was administered by the Department of Indian Affairs, a branch of the federal government. The Department appointed Indian agents for different parts of the country. The agents had the authority to control the lives of Aboriginal peoples in many ways. They enforced the rules of the act.

The details of the Indian Act have changed over the years, but it remains the law. It is still administered by the same department, now called Indian and Northern Affairs Canada.

Reserves

Another way the newcomers tried to change the Aboriginal peoples was to force them to give up their lands. Before the Europeans came, Aboriginal peoples had free use of all the land. Some of the people raised crops, but most lived by fishing and hunting and collecting wild fruits.

Europeans did not live this way. They lived in towns or on farms. They did not approve of the Aboriginal peoples' style of life. They thought that people should settle in one place and become farmers.

The government set aside small areas of land, or reserves, for the First Nations people. Other people are not allowed to settle, hunt, or fish on a reserve without the permission of the First Nations.

Today in Canada many people still live on reserves.

Making Masks

For some First Nations people on the coast of British Columbia, the right to hunt and fish in certain areas belonged to a family and was handed down from generation to generation. Along with this right came special songs, dances, names, and other ceremonies. All of these were considered to be possessions—things that belonged to someone.

Masks are some of the coastal peoples most valued possessions. They are worn at many of the ceremonies. Artists carve the masks from wood and decorate them with designs. Sometimes the designs are birds or animals. Sometimes they are creatures from the world of the spirits. Each mask has a special meaning for the person who owns it. It belongs to that person and cannot be used by anyone else without permission.

Try This

Design a mask for yourself. It might have round, hollow eyes, or bright-red eyebrows, or a grinning mouth. It's up to you. Think about your family. Do you have special things you like to do or special places you like to go? Can you think of a design that might have special meaning in your own case?

This is a sun mask from the Kwakwaka'wakw [kwoh-KWAH-kah-wahkw] people of coastal British Columbia.

The Residential Schools

Long ago, Aboriginal children didn't go to school. They learned about their culture in other ways. Aboriginal peoples passed on their traditions in stories, songs, and ceremonies. Children watched what their parents did, listened to the stories that the Elders told, and took part in ceremonies.

European settlers thought that the Aboriginal peoples should be taught in school. The government set up a system of **residential schools** for young Aboriginal students. They were called *residential* because the students lived at the schools, away from their families. Students were not allowed to speak their Aboriginal languages at these schools. They were also forced to give up their cultures.

There are no residential schools any longer. Aboriginal children go to school with everyone else.

In The Words Of...

Shirley Sterling

Shirley Sterling is a First Nations writer and teacher from British Columbia. She wrote a book called My Name is Seepeetza *about her own experiences at a residential school. In it, she describes a day at the school.*

At school we get up at six o'clock every morning. As soon as sister rings the bell, we kneel on the floor and say our prayers. Then we get up and take turns washing and brushing our teeth. We're not allowed to talk. When we are dressed in our uniforms, Sister marches us in lines two by two to chapel for Mass.

After Mass we put our smocks over our uniforms and line up for breakfast in the hall outside the dining room. We get gooey mush with powder milk and brown sugar. We say grace before and after every meal.

After breakfast we have jobs to do like clean the lavatories or dust the halls and sweep stairs. After our jobs are finished we put our smocks in our closets and line up in the rec room to go to class.

After school we change into our own clothes, usually jeans and blouses. Then Sister sends us outside, even if it's cold, and everybody gets an apple.

Supper is usually cabbage stew, two slices of bread with margarine, and wrinkled apples for dessert. Friday night is my favourite because we get oatmeal cookies for dessert.

Excerpt from *My Name Is Seepeetza* Text copyright © 1992 by Shirley Sterling. First published in Canada by Groundwood Books/Douglas & McIntyre. Reprinted by permission of the publisher.

Think For Yourself

Compare residential schools with your own school. What are the similarities and differences?

Use a Venn diagram like the one shown here to make your comparison. You may want to start by putting the similarities in the middle.

My School

Both

Residential School

1. ____
2. ____
3. ____

1. ____
2. ____
3. ____

1. ____
2. ____
3. ____

These photographs show a residential school in Saskatchewan. Identify ways that the Aboriginal students are being assimilated into a new culture.

A Closer Look

The Potlatch

The potlatch was one of the ceremonies that the government wanted to stop when it tried to assimilate the Aboriginal peoples. Potlatches were very special events for the First Nations who lived on the coast of British Columbia.

Potlatches celebrated special moments in the life of the community. They were held to honour someone who had died, to celebrate a wedding, to raise a totem pole, or to name a new chief. These are just some of the reasons.

In the old days, a potlatch might last several days, even weeks. There was feasting and dancing, and people gave speeches. Guests received presents from the host to thank them for being there to witness the event.

The potlatch was a way of recording history. Guests returned to their own communities and told the people there what had taken place. Events were remembered and the details were handed on in stories to younger generations. In an **oral culture**, the potlatch was an important way of preserving a record of events.

When Europeans arrived, they didn't understand the potlatch. They didn't know how important it was to the First Nations. To Europeans, giving away possessions was wasteful. They also thought the potlatch took time away from more important activities. They wanted the Aboriginal peoples to give up their traditions and assimilate into the new society. As a result, in 1884 the government passed a law that made the potlatch illegal.

The potlatch remained against the law for many years. The coastal First Nations still held their celebrations, but in secret so that they wouldn't be sent to jail. In the end, the government decided the law was unjust. In 1951, the potlatch became legal again.

Today, the potlatch remains an important ceremony for some First Nations people in British Columbia.

Try This

The potlatch was an issue that divided First Nations people and European settlers. This chart shows you the two points of view. You can make a copy of the chart. Then fill in the reasons why each side had the opinions it did.

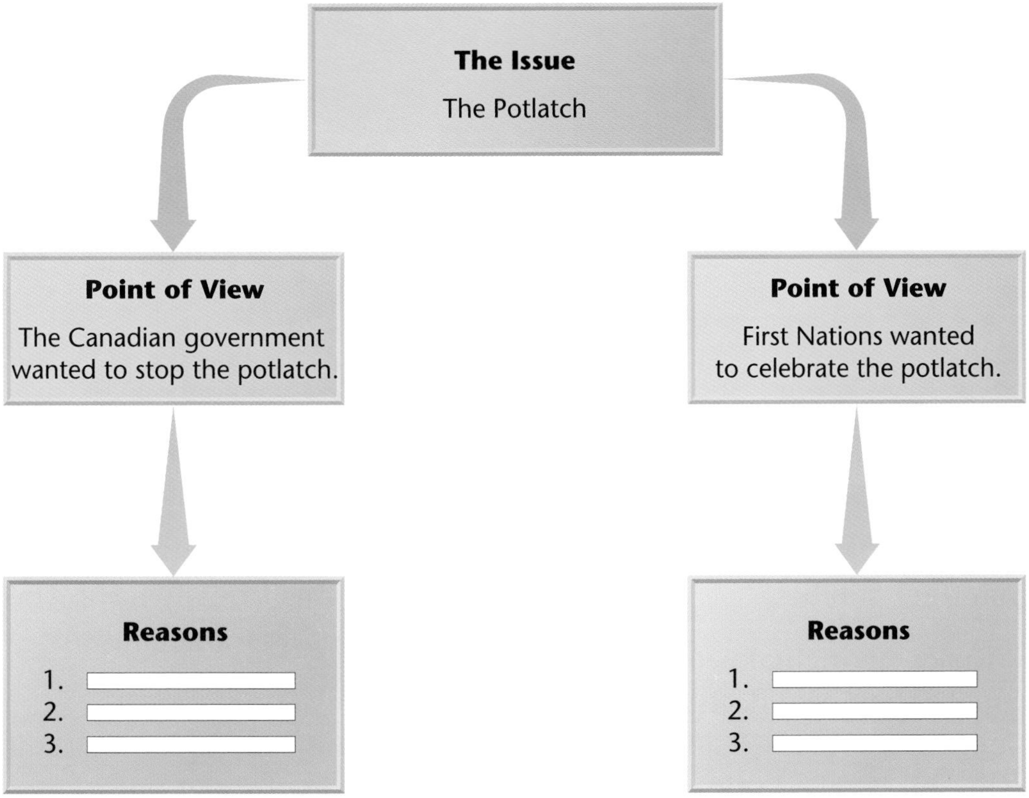

An **oral culture** is a culture without a written language. Oral cultures preserve their histories in art and in stories, rather than in books.

The Issue

The Potlatch

Point of View

The Canadian government wanted to stop the potlatch.

Point of View

First Nations wanted to celebrate the potlatch.

Reasons

1.
2.
3.

Reasons

1.
2.
3.

Self-Government

Write out your idea of what you think *self-government* means.

What do you think the term *Aboriginal self-government* means? Perhaps you have heard this term used on the news or read about it in newspapers.

For many years, Aboriginal peoples were not allowed to follow their own traditions. Many customs, such as the potlatch, were banned. Children were sent to residential schools far away from their families.

Today, Aboriginal peoples want to make their own decisions about things that will affect their lives. This is called **self-government**. Aboriginal peoples will still be part of Canada, but they will have more control over their affairs.

A kind of self-government already exists in many Aboriginal communities. Many communities are like local governments. They operate their own schools and health services. In the territory of Nunavut, created in 1999, Inuit are the majority and they control the government.

Aboriginal peoples say that self-government is not something that they want the government to give them. They say that it is a right that they already have. They just want other Canadians to recognize it.

There are many questions still to be answered about self-government. It may take different forms in different parts of the country. What is important is that Aboriginal peoples are gaining more control over their own lives.

REAL PEOPLE: ROSEMARIE KUPTANA

Rosemarie Kuptana [Koop-TAH-nuh] is an Inuit from the North. She was born out on the ice where her parents were hunting.

After going to a residential school, she went to work as a radio broadcaster. Her special interest was in programs that told about Inuit traditions. She has hosted her own radio show and has also produced programs in Inuktitut, the language of the Inuit.

Rosemarie Kuptana took part in talks with the government that led to the creation of Nunavut. One newspaper called her a "Mother of Confederation" for her work on Nunavut.

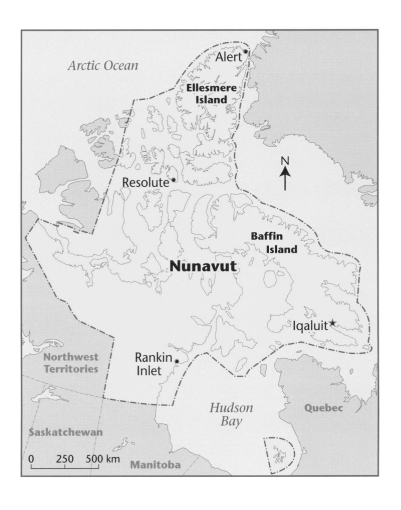

Explain the term *Mother of Confederation.*

The new territory of Nunavut was created on 1 April 1999. Nunavut's land is made up of the central and eastern parts of the Northwest Territories. This land has been the ancestral home of the Inuit for thousands of years. The Inuit are now shaping their new government according to their own culture, traditions, and goals.

Find Out

Invite a member of a First Nation in your community to visit your class. Ask your visitor about the history and traditions of his or her First Nation. Also ask about self-government. How would self-government change things for the local First Nation? How would it change things for your community?

After your visitor leaves, write out your understanding of what he or she said self-government means. You can use an issue chart like the one shown here to help you organize your understanding.

Step 1
The Issue

Self-government

Step 2
Point of View

What does the visitor say about self-government?

Step 3
Reasons

The visitor thinks this way because:
1.
2.
3.

Have your own ideas about self-government changed since you began studying the subject? Look back at what you wrote earlier about self-government. In what way would you change what you wrote?

Looking Back

In this chapter, you learned about the relationship over the years between government and Aboriginal peoples in Canada. You also began to discover what Aboriginal peoples are doing to regain control of their affairs.

Why is it important for people to be able to make their own decisions?

Chapter 7

Canadian Communities

*I*f you are like most Canadians, you live in a **community**. Cities, towns, and villages are all examples of communities.

Communities are places where a lot of businesses and activities are located. If you live in the countryside or on a farm, your community probably has a business area where you shop, meet friends, or go to school. What are the many things you can do in the community where you live?

In this chapter, you can find out why different Canadian communities are located where they are. You can also learn how to find these communities on a map. Think about all the activities that go on in any community.

Images of Community

O n pages 101 to 102, you'll find images of six Canadian communities. Some show the communities as they look today. Others show them as they looked in the past.

Try This

Study the images on pages 101 to 102. Use these pictures and a map of Canada to practise gathering and sorting information.

In Chapter 1, you learned that Canada has several different regions. Make a list of these regions. Using a map of Canada in your atlas, locate each of the communities shown in the pictures. Place the name of the community beside the region in which it is located.

List all the means of transportation shown in the pictures under two headings: Modern and Old-fashioned. Which means of transportation do you consider to be modern? Which do you think are old-fashioned? Explain the main difference between these two means of transportation.

For each picture, make a **hypothesis** [hy-POTH-uh-sis] about how the landscape might have influenced people to settle in this area. For example, perhaps the Tsimshian [TSIM-shee-un] village was next to the water because the people used to travel on water.

Your **hypothesis** is your first idea about why something is the way it is. When you make a hypothesis, you do not know for certain that it is true. You are making a suggestion based on what you already know. A hypothesis is the beginning for further investigation.

This painting, called *Tracks and Traffic*, shows the railway yards in Toronto. It was painted in 1912 by J. E. H. Macdonald, an Ontario artist. What ideas about the city do you think Macdonald was trying to present?

An **aerial photograph** is a photograph taken from the air, usually from an airplane.

This is an **aerial** [AIR-ee-ul] **photograph** of downtown Calgary. What is the advantage of this type of photograph in identifying landscape features?

This is a painting of a small town called Silver Plains. Based on the landscape, in what region of the country do you think the town is located? What economic activity do you think takes place here?

The community of Herring Neck is one of many **outport** villages in Newfoundland. An outport is a small community on the coast. What economic activity do you think goes on here?

This painting is called *Cobalt*. It was made in 1931 by the Toronto artist Yvonne McKague. Judging by the landscape, what kind of economic activity would you say went on in the town?

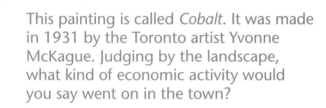

Gordon Miller painted the village of Gitsaex on the Skeena River in British Columbia. The people living here belonged to the Tsimshian First Nation. Can you point out the chief's house? What are the tall poles in front of the houses called? Compared to the other communities shown on these pages, what things identify this as a First Nation community?

Welcome to Our Communities!

On the previous pages, you looked at pictures of six Canadian communities. Now it's time to think about your own community. Where is it located? Who lives there? What kind of activities go on there?

In The Words Of...

Someone Like You

Nicole Benotti is 11 years old. Here she talks about the community where she lives.

Hi, my name is Nicole Benotti. My friends call me Nicky. I'm in grade five. And guess what? My mother is my teacher this year. It can be pretty embarrassing sometimes!

I live in Powell River. It's a city on the west coast of British Columbia. You have to take two ferry rides to drive here from Vancouver.

My grandfather came here from Italy. He came to work in the paper mill. Lots of Italians did. The paper mill is where a lot of people in town work, including my dad. It's at the edge of town. You can see the big cloud of steam coming out of the smokestack. People say they can smell the mill in the air, but I guess I must be used to it.

My dad says that Powell River is a port. That means that huge freighters come here from around the world to load paper from the mill.

On weekends we go fishing for salmon in our boat. That's one of the coolest things about living on the coast. You can go right down to the water anytime you want. Sometimes I walk along the dock and watch the fishers unloading the crabs and prawns and stuff that they catch.

This is the site of the paper mill in Powell River.

Quick Facts about Powell River:

- It has a population of 13 131.
- It was established in 1910.
- It was named for an early government official, Israel Wood Powell.
- Forestry is the major industry.
- At one time, the paper mill was the largest in the world.

Work and Play

People are attracted to the places where they live for many different reasons. One important reason is that they can find jobs there. This is what brought Nicole's grandfather to Powell River.

Of course, people don't work all the time. We all have spare time that we like to spend doing things we enjoy with our friends and family. People may choose to live in a community because it offers many different leisure activities.

Try This

Compare the community where you live to Powell River. You can use a chart like the one shown here.

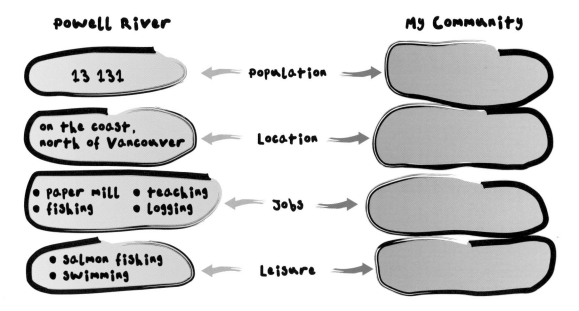

Powell River — My Community

Powell River		My Community
13 131	Population	
on the coast, north of Vancouver	Location	
• paper mill • teaching • fishing • logging	Jobs	
• salmon fishing • swimming	Leisure	

Based on your comparison, what do you think is the most important difference between your community and Powell River? Are there ways in which the two communities are similar? Explain the similarities.

Find Out

To learn about the businesses in your community, look at an issue of the local newspaper. List all the businesses that advertise in the paper. If you live in a big city, perhaps you'll want to list only businesses of a certain kind: clothing stores or factories, for example.

Draw a simple street map of your community. Mark each business on your map.

When you have completed your map, examine it. Is there a neighbourhood in your community where many of the businesses are located? What do you think are the reasons for this? You might want to visit the neighbourhood to get some ideas. Or invite the owner of a business to visit your class to explain why the business is located where it is.

Where in the World?

The parallel of latitude that circles the middle of the globe is called the Equator. It divides the earth in half. The northern half is known as the Northern Hemisphere and the southern half is known as the Southern Hemisphere. The Equator is at 0 degrees. It is the starting point for numbering the other parallels.

How would you find Powell River? Using the description given to you by Nicole, try to find her community on a map of Canada. She told you that Powell River is in British Columbia. She also said that it was on the seacoast and it was north of Vancouver. So its location should be easy to find.

There is another way to find places on the map, using just numbers and letters. Every place in the world can be located if you know its **latitude** and **longitude** [LON-juh-tood].

These children are drawing lines of latitude and longitude on a circle that represents the globe.

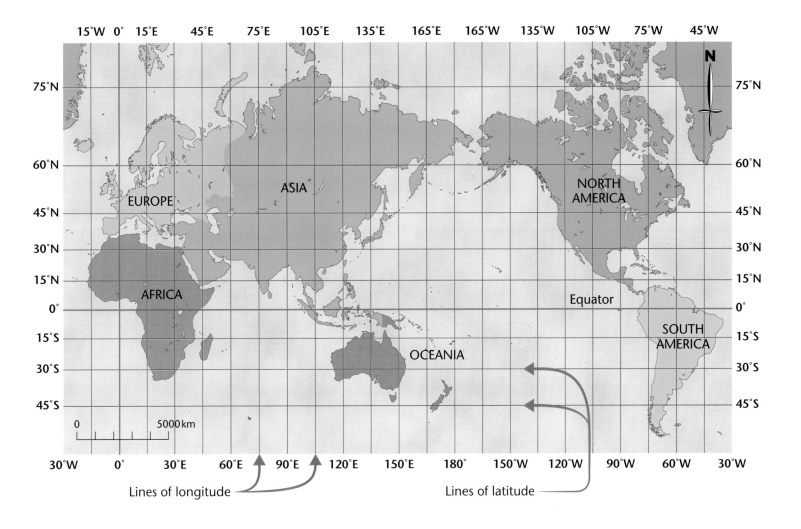

Latitude and longitude are imaginary lines traced on a map. Draw a circle on a piece of paper. Imagine that circle is the globe. If you draw lines from the top of the circle to the bottom, these are lines of longitude. They are also called **meridians** of longitude.

Now draw some straight lines across the circle. These are lines of latitude, also called **parallels** of latitude.

Map-makers divide the globe into 360 lines, or degrees, of longitude. Because so many of the scientists who developed this system lived in England, it was decided to make the 0 meridian the one that runs through Greenwich [GREN-ich], England.

All the meridians to the west of Greenwich are numbered as degrees of west longitude. All the meridians to the east of Greenwich are numbered as degrees of east longitude. On the other side of the world, where the two sets of meridians meet, is the 180-degree meridian.

The pattern that is formed by the lines of longitude and latitude is called a **grid**. A grid is a way of using numbers and letters to locate a place on a map.

Parallels of latitude are also numbered in degrees. There are 90 parallels between the Equator and the North Pole, which is 90 degrees north. There are another 90 parallels between the Equator and the South Pole, which is 90 degrees south.

To make things even more precise, each degree of latitude and longitude is divided again into 60 minutes. For example, a location might be at longitude 157° 52" W, meaning 157 degrees and 52 minutes west of Greenwich. Or it might be at latitude 32° 15" S, meaning 32 degrees and 15 minutes south of the Equator.

Using latitude and longitude, it is possible to find any location on a map of the world.

Try This

Test your knowledge of latitude and longitude by trying to find Vancouver and Powell River on a map.

First of all, we have to know the numbers for both cities. Most atlases will have this information. Vancouver is at latitude 49° 15" N and longitude 123° 10" W. Powell River is at latitude 49° 54" N and longitude 124° 34" W.

On a map of British Columbia or of Canada, locate the line of latitude for Powell River. Then find the line of longitude. Powell River should be on the map where the two lines meet.

Repeat the same steps to locate Vancouver.

Now that you have found Vancouver and Powell River, why not try to locate your own community? Find out its longitude and latitude, then pinpoint it on a map of Canada.

Find Out

Use a map of Canada to answer the following questions:

- *What parallel of latitude forms the border between British Columbia and the United States?*

- *What meridian of longitude forms the border between Alberta and Saskatchewan?*

- *What city is at latitude 44° 38" N and longitude 63° 35" W?*

- *What is the latitude and longitude for the six communities pictured on pages 101 to 102?*

In 1932, Waterton Park in Alberta and Glacier National Park in Montana became known as the Glacier-Waterton International Peace Park. This photograph shows a Canada-US border crossing in the park.

Why Are We Here?

Have you ever wondered why your community is located where it is? After all, communities do not appear by accident. There are reasons why people choose to develop a community at one spot instead of another.

Military Defence

Military defence is one reason that communities might be located where they are. Let's look at a couple of examples. In 1858, when British Columbia was created, officials were going to locate the capital up the Fraser River near Fort Langley, the salmon and fur-trading post. The new capital was going to be called Derby. The land was **surveyed** and lots were sold.

But Derby turned out to have problems. The site was located on low land beside the river. A well-travelled trail led south to the United States. Relations between Canada and the US were not as friendly as they are today. Some people worried that the new capital would be open to attack if war broke out with the Americans.

Farther west was another site. It was on the opposite side of the river, so it was protected from an attack by the Americans. There was a high hill giving a clear view of the surrounding countryside. There was also a deep harbour for boats using the river. For all these reasons, officials changed their minds and decided to set up the capital at this new site instead of at Derby.

The new community was called Queensborough. We know it today as New Westminster. It is no longer the capital of British Columbia, but it is still an important community.

Quebec City's location also provided good military defence. Perched high on a cliff above the St. Lawrence River, soldiers could protect New France from invasion.

Transportation

Another factor that helps to explain the location of a

> When land is **surveyed**, it is measured in order to make maps or plans of the area.

community is transportation. Communities have to be located where people can reach them. For this reason, many communities in Canada are found near rivers or lakes. In the early days, before highways and railways, most transportation was by water. The capital of every province in Canada is located on a river or a lake or in an ocean harbour.

Jobs

People also prefer to live close to where they can find jobs. Some communities, such as Powell River, are surrounded by forests. So logging is an important activity for people who live there. Other towns are located close to mines or oil fields. On the coast of British Columbia, communities developed for fishers and their families.

Transportation, jobs, defence—these are all good reasons to explain why a community is located where it is. Can you think of any others? Perhaps it's time to find out about your own community.

Reading Hint

When you start to read a new section, sometimes it helps to read the headings and look at the pictures first. This gives you an idea of what the section is about before you start reading in detail.

This view of Quebec City from the Citadel was painted in 1836 by P. J. Bainbridge.

Learning about Your Community's History

Every community has a history. Sometimes we think that history is something that happens only to other people, not to ourselves. Our own lives are too ordinary, we think.

But that is not true. History is something that happens to everyone. It is about what happens in your community just as much as it is about the great events of war and politics.

It shouldn't be difficult to find out the story of your community. Perhaps there are books written about it. There may be a local museum with displays about the past. Sometimes the local library has old photographs showing the community as it used to be. People who are interested in community history may have formed a historical society to carry out research of their own.

One good way of gathering information is to talk to the older people who have lived in your community for a long time. They will be able to share their memories with you.

These are all sources of information for your research.

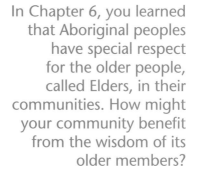

In Chapter 6, you learned that Aboriginal peoples have special respect for the older people, called Elders, in their communities. How might your community benefit from the wisdom of its older members?

HOW TO... Carry Out an Interview

When you talk to older people about their memories, it's best to do so as a formal interview. Take notes during the interview to remind yourself later what was said. You don't have to copy down everything, just the main points.

When you are ready to begin, follow these steps:

1. Find the best people to interview. Choose those who are healthy, who have good memories, and who have lived in the community for a long time.

2. Make sure that they understand the purpose of the interview. People will give the most information when they know why they are being asked.

3. Do some research ahead of time so you will know what kind of questions to ask. Don't just say, "Tell me about your life." Most people won't know where to begin. It's better to focus your questions. For example, "What do you remember about the first automobile in town?" or "What was it like working in the sawmill?"

4. Prepare a list of about five questions before the interview. You don't want to forget anything in the middle of the interview!

5. When you have finished your interview, think of a way to share the information with your classmates.

Many communities in Canada began as trading posts.

Find Out

Research the history of your community. Start by making a list of basic questions. Here are two questions to get you started:

- *When was your community created?*

- *What were, and are, its major industries?*

Develop your own questions, and do some research to find the answers.

When you've answered these questions, produce a museum-style exhibit in your classroom about the history of your community. Draw a mural showing some important events. Display photographs of old buildings or important people. Put up posters with interesting information. These are just three ideas. What else could you include in your exhibit?

When your exhibit is ready, you might want to invite other classes in your school to visit your classroom.

Looking Back

In this chapter, you learned about Canadian communities. You looked at your own community and researched its history. You also improved your map skills by learning about longitude and latitude.

Why do you think most people choose to live in communities?

Chapter 8

Transportation and Communications

How did you arrive at school this morning? Did you walk or ride your bicycle? Did someone give you a ride in a car? Walking, biking, and driving are all forms of transportation.

Now imagine that you are going on holiday. Perhaps you're going to visit relatives in another province. Perhaps you're going camping in the mountains. How will you get there? Many people travel by car. If you're going a long distance, you'll probably fly in an airplane or take the bus or train.

In this chapter, you'll learn about the different ways that Canadians have travelled and communicated with one another.

Moving Around

Futuristic means looking forward to the future.

On pages 116 to 118, you'll find pictures of different ways of travelling. Some are old-fashioned and no longer in use. Others are up-to-date, even **futuristic**.

This painting shows the sailing vessel *William D. Lawrence*. It was 75 metres long, the largest sailing ship ever built in Nova Scotia. The *Lawrence* was one of many sailing ships built in the Maritime provinces in the 1870s and 1880s. This period is known as the Age of Sail, when Maritimers were producing the finest wooden sailing ships in the world. Since the ships were made of wood, what other industry was supported by shipbuilding?

This painting, by Robert Whale, shows a railway train at Niagara Falls in about 1870. Where is Niagara Falls? The first railways were being built in Canada at this time. Why do you think the artist put the falls and the railway together in the same painting?

A line of Red River carts crosses the plains in a painting by William Hind in 1862. The Métis people used Red River carts to haul their possessions. The carts were made of wood. When the wheels were strapped underneath, the carts could float across rivers like a raft. What were the disadvantages of Red River carts in the rainy season or in winter?

Snowmobiles are used for transportation over snow and ice. What form of transportation has the snowmobile largely replaced in Canada's North?

Frances Hopkins travelled across Canada with a group of fur-trade canoes in the 1860s. If you look closely, you can see her sitting among the paddlers. What made the canoe so well suited to the fur trade?

The Canadarm is a remote-controlled arm used by astronauts to move objects around in space. It was invented by Canadian scientists. Space-ships are used to explore outer space. What forms of transportation shown on pages 116 to 117 were used to explore Canada?

Try This

As time passed, some of the forms of transportation pictured on pages 116 to 118 became out of date. The sailing ship was replaced by the steamship. Horse-drawn wagons were replaced by motor-driven vehicles.

Make a timeline that shows the forms of transportation in the order in which they were used. At the beginning of the line, show the earliest form of transportation. At the end of the line, show the most modern form. Show the other forms in between.

Think of reasons why one form of transportation replaced an earlier form. Make a list of these reasons.

Think For Yourself

Make your own drawing of a form of transportation that is not pictured on pages 116 to 118.

Have you chosen a form that is still being used? Or have you chosen a form from the past or the future? If it's from the past, why is it no longer in use? If it's still in use, can you think of a form of transportation that might replace it in the future?

Between 1908 and 1927, the American automaker Henry Ford produced over 15 million copies of his Model T Ford.

Find Out

The railway brought important changes to life in Canada when it was introduced in the 19th century. In the same way, the automobile brought important changes in the 20th century.

Do a research project on these two forms of transportation. The library has many books about trains and automobiles. Focus your research on the important question of changes to society.

Compare these changes by making two lists—one for the railway and one for the automobile. Indicate which changes you think were good and which turned out to be bad. Support your opinions with facts and examples.

Discuss your list with your classmates and see where you agree and disagree.

People and Places

Transportation means moving things from place to place. This can include people who are travelling to see friends and family. It can also include freight that is being hauled from the factory to the customers. Or it can include information that is being carried, perhaps by mail or a courier service.

Canada is a huge country, the second largest in the world. Because of this size, transportation has always been a challenge for Canadians. We have had to move things across long distances.

In pioneer days, transportation was difficult and expensive. People mostly used the waterways, travelling down the rivers and across the lakes. But in winter, these waterways freeze over. Then how did transportation take place?

Even in modern times, bad weather can make transportation difficult. Snowstorms shut down the airports. High winds keep the ferries from venturing out. Heavy rain causes mudslides that block the highways.

On the Move

Think for a moment about the many products that you use during a day. Where do they come from? When you get up in the morning, you might put on clothes that were made in China. You might eat oranges from California for breakfast. Your family's car might come from Japan.

All these products, and many more, have to be carried to your community by some method of transportation. Many years ago, they may have arrived by canoe or steamboat. Today they come by railway, truck, and ocean-going freighter.

Without these methods of transportation, distant parts of the country and of the world would not be able to do business with each other. We would have to rely on the very limited number of things that we could make for ourselves.

We rely on different methods of transportation to supply us with the things we need.

Think For Yourself

Transportation is an important influence in peoples' lives. Think about the changes brought about by different methods of transportation. Each new method made it possible to do things that had not been possible to do before.

For each of the methods of transportation shown in the photos on pages 116 to 118, complete the following sentence: *"After the invention of the sailing ship (or railway, and so on), people could . . . "*

The Great Ice Storm of 1998 shut down large areas of Eastern Canada, in some cases for several weeks.

Railway Across Canada

Have you ever taken a train ride? Not so many years ago, the railway was the most important form of travel in Canada. This was before the automobile and the airplane were invented. If you wanted to get anywhere, you had to take the train.

Rail lines linked every community with the outside world. Some people even think that without the railway holding it together, Canada as a country might not have been possible.

The biggest railway of all was the Canadian Pacific. It was the first line built across Canada from Ontario to British Columbia. Another branch ran east to Nova Scotia.

Working on the Railway

The men in the photograph on page 123 are standing with their tools beside the railway track at a place in British Columbia. The next day, 7 November 1885, the bosses will be there for the official opening of the line. Donald Smith, Lord Strathcona, will hammer a silver spike into the ground. It will be called the Last Spike because it is the last of many spikes that have gone into building the line. William C. Van Horne will declare that the Canadian Pacific Railway across Canada is finished.

Early trains were pulled by steam locomotives like this one.

On this day, it is the turn of the men who have worked on the railway. For ten years, they have been building the line across the swamps and through the mountains. They have cut and hauled wooden ties. They have laid down the ties and fastened steel rails across them. Now people and freight are able to cross Canada from one ocean to the other.

The railway means a great deal to people in Canada. Towns will spring up along the route where none existed before. Travellers will be able to see the country from one end to the other for the first time. Immigrant settlers can now reach the interior and begin farming the land.

Where the train tracks end, the docks begin. Now goods can cross the Pacific Ocean by ship and be loaded onto the train in Vancouver. From there, they can travel across Canada by rail, be loaded again onto a ship in Halifax, and travel to Europe. Businesses and farmers in Canada will be able to ship their goods to markets far away, even around the world.

British Columbia became a province of Canada in 1871. In return, Canada agreed to build a railway across the western plains and over the Rocky Mountains to the Pacific, joining the two ends of the country. The result was the Canadian Pacific Railway, completed in 1885. Think about all the different landscapes in Canada. What major problems would the railway builders have faced?

Think For Yourself

Imagine you are one of the people in the photograph on page 123. You have been working for years to complete the railway, and now the day has come. Write a letter home to your parents telling them about the project and sharing your feelings about it. Explain to them why the railway is being built.

Builders of the Railway

The railway was built in large part by immigrant workers. On the Prairies, they came mostly from European countries such as Norway, Finland, and Italy. As you discovered in Chapter 3, many workers in British Columbia came from China.

Workers were paid about a dollar a day. Chinese workers got even less. If they got sick or if bad weather kept them off the job, they weren't paid at all. They lived in dingy log houses beside the track and ate a diet of salt pork, corned beef, molasses, beans, and tea. In summer, the heat was intense. The biting insects settled in clouds around the men. In winter, the cold sliced through their clothes.

If they were ill, there were no doctors and nurses to help them. Many workers were killed on the job or died of disease. They lie buried in unmarked graves beside the track.

These railway workers posed with the cook outside his railway car in Saskatchewan in 1903.

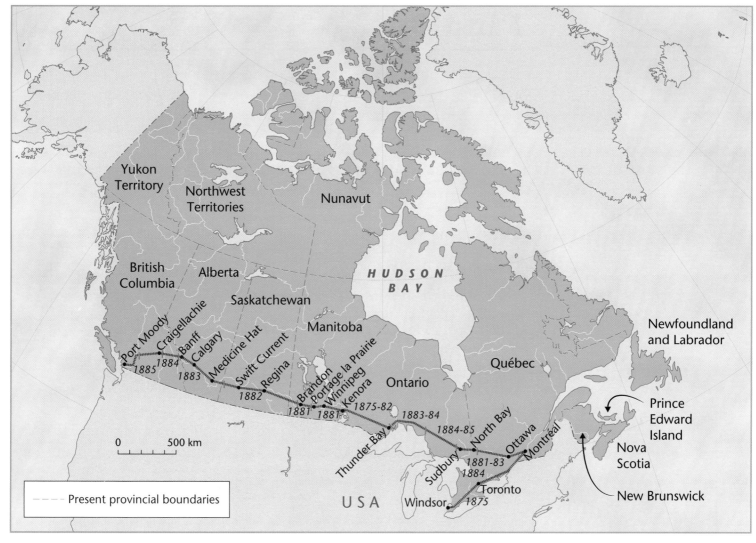

This map shows the route followed by the Canadian Pacific Railway across Canada. Notice that many communities are located on the line. Towns tended to spring up where the railway passed. Other towns located away from the track often faded away. Explain why the railway was so important to the survival of a community.

The Railway Today

The railway is still an important method of transportation. Looking out from the window of a train is a wonderful way to see Canada.

But fewer people have the time to take long train trips any more. Fast as it is, the train is much slower than an airplane. It takes almost four days to travel by train from Vancouver to Montreal. Do you know how long it takes to fly the same distance in an airplane?

For many trips, it is more convenient to drive a car or take a bus. At the same time, trains are still a good way to carry freight. Nowadays the railway is used more for freight than for passengers.

Find Out

What are the different ways of travelling across Canada today? Make a list. Don't forget that bicycles are a form of transportation, too. Many people like to cycle across the country.

When you have completed your list, choose one form of transportation and think about its advantages and disadvantages. For example, it may be

- fast

- expensive

- the most comfortable

- quite harmful to the environment

Present your ideas in a doughnut chart like the one shown here.

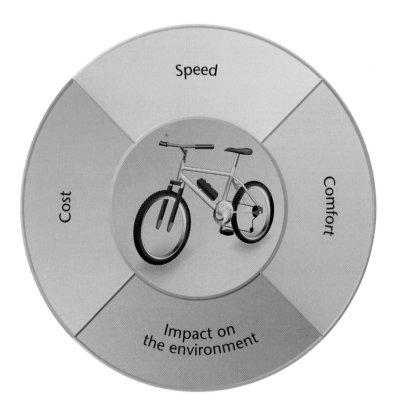

Keeping in Touch

You have learned that transportation is about moving people and things. But it is also about moving ideas and information. This kind of movement is called communications.

You receive a letter from a friend in Toronto. On your birthday, a courier may bring a package from your favourite aunt in Saskatchewan. You telephone a classmate to discuss homework. You e-mail your cousin in a distant city. These are all ways that you keep in touch with people you care about. They all involve different ways of communicating.

Canadians keep in touch with each other so that we know what is going on in other parts of the country. We want to know what life is like for other Canadians. We can find out by reading the newspaper and watching the news on television. In what other ways can we keep in touch?

Without communications, it would be much more difficult for Canadians to learn about events in the rest of the country.

Today, people receive much of their information about the world by watching television.

13 September 1787

Dear Roderic:

I have been waiting here for Mr. McGillivray's Brigade since September 5. He arrived yesterday. To my great surprise, Barrieu did not come with him. I am afraid Barrieu has had an accident. Because he did not catch up with the other canoes, they had to wait several days. I hope that if he is alive he will be sent after me immediately. I cannot do without the things that are in his canoe. I will wait for him for two or three days farther on. So, if Barrieu is lost, I beg that someone else who knows the road would follow me with the canoe I need.

Adapted from W. Kaye Lamb, ed., *The Journals and Letters of Sir Alexander Mackenzie* (Cambridge: Cambridge University Press, 1970).

The Changing World of Communications

More than 200 years ago, the explorer and fur trader Alexander Mackenzie was travelling by canoe in the Northwest. He wrote the above letter to his cousin, Roderic Mackenzie. Alexander gave the letter to one of the men who worked for him to carry to his cousin by canoe.

As you can see, Alexander is in trouble because he doesn't know what has happened to one of his canoes. The only way he can find out is to send a letter that will take several days to reach its destination. It will take several more days to get a response. He can't phone Roderic, because the telephone hasn't been invented yet. For the same reason, he can't e-mail him or send a fax.

Think of the many ways that people communicate with each other. E-mail is one of the newest ways of communicating. How does e-mail make it easier to keep in touch? Why do you think it is important to be able to communicate quickly with other people?

In those days, writing a letter was the only way people could keep in touch over long distances. If you sent a letter to someone in a faraway community, it might take weeks to arrive. If you lived in Victoria in 1858 and sent a letter to someone in England, it would take months to arrive. It had to travel around the world by sailing ship.

How different things are now! Almost everywhere in the world, people who are far away from each other can be in touch in seconds. Marta, who lives in the Czech Republic, comes to visit relatives in Canada. She phones her mother to let her know that she has arrived safely. She sends a postcard to a teammate on her volleyball team. She sends an e-mail to another friend, telling about her trip. Marta has many ways of communicating.

Media is a Latin word. It is the plural of *medium*. A medium is a means by which something is communicated. Media are the different means by which information is spread. Examples of media are books, newspapers, radio, television, and billboards. Can you think of any other examples?

People receive much more information about the world than they used to. The Internet provides users with instant information. At the end of 1998, there were over 150 million people using the Internet around the world. By the year 2005, there will be close to 720 million users.

Sending the News

Telephones, fax machines, and e-mail are ways that people keep in touch with each other. There is another kind of communication that keeps you in touch with your community and the world. This kind of communication is called the **media**.

Many years ago, people got most of their information from the newspaper. Newspapers were the only medium for spreading the news. Nowadays, people receive news from many media.

How many different media do you use in a single day? Many people read a newspaper in the morning, listen to the radio at work, watch the news on television, and use the Internet after supper.

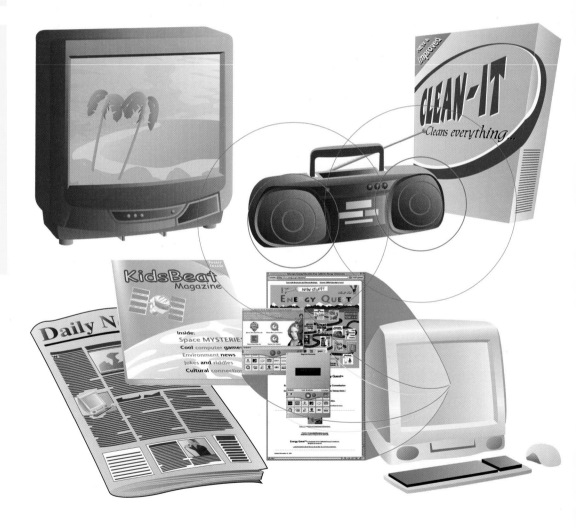

A Closer Look

Bias

With so much information in the world, how can we tell what is true and what is not true? We used to believe everything that we read in a newspaper or saw on television. Now we are learning that some of the things we see and read may be **biased**. That is, they may be expressing an unfair opinion based on very little information. A fair opinion is based on evidence—facts and examples that provide information. In order to form a fair opinion, people need to consider the evidence and decide for themselves.

We all have opinions. You may like one kind of vegetable better than another. You may prefer a movie you saw last week over the one you saw last night. These are personal choices. Everyone makes them.

Opinions become important when they influence the information you are receiving. Here are two versions of the same story. Imagine they are being read on television by newscasters. As you read them, watch for words and phrases that indicate a biased opinion.

"It was a sad sight today as loggers cut down a forest on the outskirts of town. People shouted in protest as the logging machines moved in to complete the job. 'Save our forest!' shouted one woman as she waved a placard in the air."

"It was a hopeful sight today as loggers set to work cutting down a forest on the outskirts of town. The logging means jobs for 50 people and a real boost to the local economy. A few demonstrators turned out to protest, but they were ignored by the loggers."

Think For Yourself

In the account on page 131, how do you think the first newscaster feels about the logging? What about the second newscaster?

List the words from both newscasts that express opinions about the logging. Do the words express a good opinion or a bad opinion?

Try This

Imagine you are a news writer at the local television station. Prepare a brief news report about the logging story on page 131. First, prepare a report that is biased in favour of a particular point of view. Then prepare a report that attempts to be fair and express all points of view.

Play the role of a newscaster and read the reports to the class. Let the class decide which report is fairer, and why.

Looking Back

In this chapter, you looked at the importance of transportation and communications in Canada. You also learned about bias in the news media.

Why is it important to ask questions about what you see and hear in the news media?

Chapter 9

Resources and Settlement

Look around your classroom. How many things made out of paper do you see? That paper is made from trees. The legs on the desks and tables are made from metal that comes from mines. The water coming out of the tap comes from reservoirs that hold rain and melted snow.

The electricity that turns on the lights comes from power plants that run on the energy produced by running water or burning coal. The oil or gas that heats the school comes from wells deep below the ground.

All of these things are **natural resources**. They come from nature and are useful to humans. Forests, minerals, oil, and gas are all natural resources that are found in different parts of Canada. So are fish, water, and furs.

In this chapter, you can find out about some of Canada's natural resources. You'll discover that two resources were especially important in British Columbia: furs and gold.

The Resources of Canada

Canada is a country with many natural resources. Some of the resources we put to our own use. We build power plants that transform the energy from running water into electricity for our homes and industries. We cut down trees to make lumber for building. Trees and water are two common natural resources.

Other resources we **export** around the world. In British Columbia, for example, coal is exported to Japan where it is used to make steel. Lumber is exported to the United States and many other countries.

The map of Canada on page 135 shows where many resources are located.

Electricity is produced by water at power dams. Then it is carried by wires many kilometres to communities like your own.

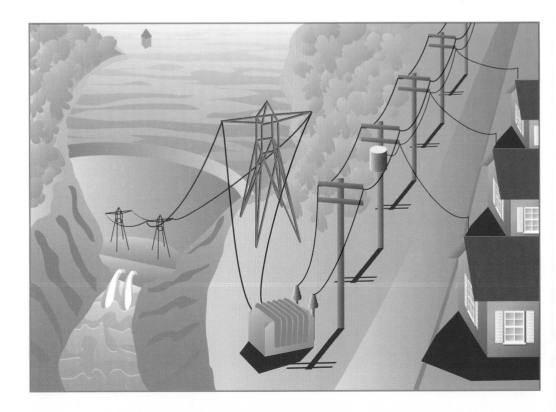

A Resource Map of Canada

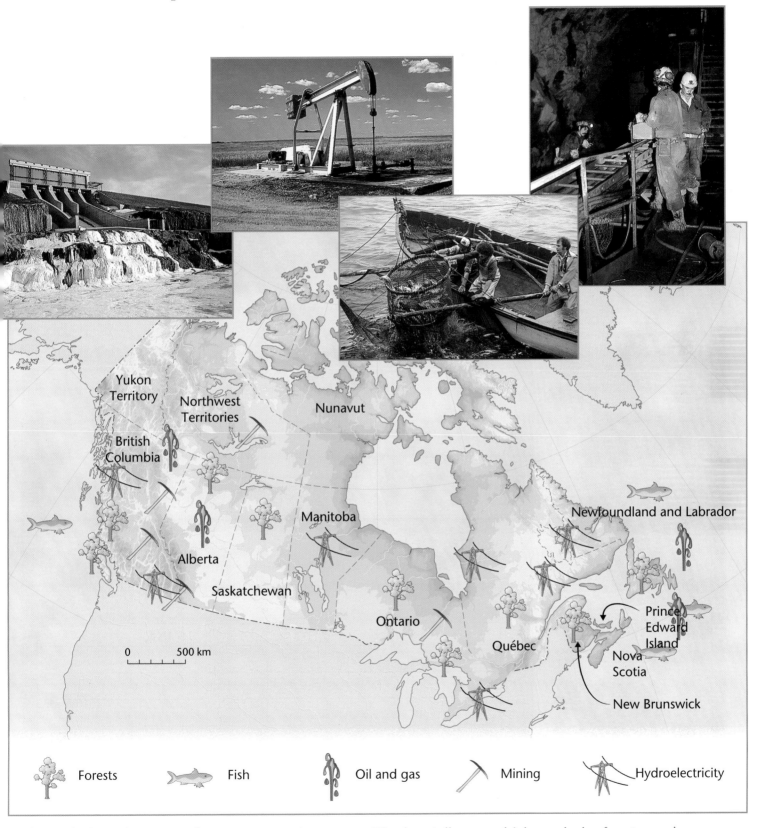

Forests

Fish

Oil and gas

Mining

Hydroelectricity

Each symbol on the map refers to a natural resource. The key tells you which symbol refers to each resource.

Try This

Study the map on page 135 carefully. Make sure you understand what each of the symbols means. Try to locate one example of each symbol on the map.

Make a list of the ten provinces of Canada. Beside each province, write the name of a natural resource that can be found there. In what parts of Canada is fishing important? Which provinces produce oil and gas?

Find Out

Find out what natural resources are found in your area. Are there mines, forests, dams, or oil wells near your community? One source of information is your local Chamber of Commerce. Contact someone there and ask about the main industries in your community. Then do more research on one of the natural resources in your area. To focus your research, you can start with these questions:

- *How long have people been making use of the resource?*
- *What is the resource used for?*
- *Who are the customers who buy the resource?*

Think For Yourself

Make a copy of the chart below. The first column of this chart shows some of Canada's natural resources. In the second column, you can fill in some of the ways each resource is used. For example, gas is used as a fuel to heat homes.

Resources	Use
water	
trees	
minerals (coal, gold, copper, and so on)	
oil and natural gas	
soil	

Can you think of any natural resources that are not included in the chart? In what ways are they put to use?

A Closer Look

Energy Resources

When you get up in the morning, the first thing you do, especially in winter, is turn on a light. It's cold outside, so you turn up the heat. That heat might come from an oil furnace, a gas furnace, or electric heating. Which do you have in your home?

Next you cook your breakfast on the gas or electric stove. Then it's off to school, perhaps by car or bus.

Just an hour out of bed, and already you have used several different forms of energy! Energy is what keeps us warm. It runs our cars, provides electricity, and lets us cook our meals.

When we feel like doing many different things, we say we have a lot of energy. That kind of energy we provide for ourselves. We jump, run, and play games and sports. But the energy we use for our homes and cars must come from somewhere else.

Canadians use five different kinds of energy resources: electricity, natural gas, oil, coal, and nuclear power. Energy resources make our lives easier and more comfortable. Sometimes, though, resources have disadvantages. They may harm the environment, or they may be dangerous to produce. For example, every year many people are killed in mining accidents. When we burn coal, it gives off chemicals that pollute the atmosphere. Hydroelectric dams may harm the salmon that migrate up and down the rivers.

Smog is another word for dirty air. It is a combination of the words *smoke* and *fog*. Smog is caused by pollution from industry and from automobiles. Breathing smog over long periods damages the lungs.

Find Out

Research and report on one of the five energy resources. Use the questions below to focus your research. There may be other questions you want to investigate.

- *Where in Canada is the resource located?*

- *How is the resource turned into energy that you use in your everyday life?*

- *What is one way that the resource damages the natural environment?*

- *Why should people use more, or less, of the resource?*

Think of a way to report your findings. For example, you could present a written report. Or you could make a poster or a mural showing what you've learned.

The Changing Need for Resources

Sometimes things change, and people don't need a resource any longer. Years ago most homes were heated by coal. Basements were full of heaps of black coal, and homeowners had to shovel it into the furnaces where it burned and gave off heat. Then along came oil, natural gas, and electricity, so people no longer had as much use for coal. It is still an important fuel for industry, but not as much for homes any more.

Someday gasoline might also be an example of a resource that we no longer need so much. Scientists are hard at work trying to develop a vehicle that will run on electricity. At the moment, exhaust fumes from cars are polluting the air that we breathe. Larger cities have serious problems with **smog**.

Electricity is a much cleaner fuel than gasoline. If cars used electricity, the air in our cities would be healthier.

In the past, trains used coal for fuel. Burning coal heated boilers of water, which produced the steam that powered the engines.

Scientists are working to replace the gasoline engine. One alternative they are developing is the electrical battery, so that a car could be plugged in for recharging. Another alternative is the fuel cell. A fuel cell turns a chemical (usually hydrogen) into electricity, which then runs the vehicle. This photograph shows a vehicle that uses a fuel cell. The leading developer of fuel cells in the world is a company in British Columbia called Ballard Power Systems.

Try This

What would be the advantages of using electricity as fuel for a car instead of gasoline? Can you think of any disadvantages? Present your ideas in a pro/con chart.

Issue: Electric Cars	
Pros	Cons
1.	1.
2.	2.
3.	3.

The Trade in Furs

Different parts of Canada have different natural resources. Fishing has always been important to people in the Atlantic provinces. On the Prairies, grain growing began with the arrival of settlers 120 years ago. Alberta produces most of Canada's oil, while northern Ontario has many large mines.

British Columbia is also rich in natural resources. Water power for electricity, fish from the oceans, coal from the ground, and timber from the forests: these are all important resources today and for the future.

This chapter looks at some of the resources that were important in the past. One of these was fur.

Otter Furs

The first resource that attracted Europeans to British Columbia was fur. In China, the United States, and Europe, fur was in great demand. It was used to make hats and coats and other items of clothing.

The best fur came from the beaver, although other animals produced fine fur as well, including the mink, the muskrat, and the fox. All these animals were plentiful in the forests of Canada, including British Columbia.

In British Columbia, there was a particular animal that attracted the attention of the traders. It was the sea otter. Sea otters live in the ocean along the coast,

Sea otters were in such demand by the traders that they were all wiped out on the BC coast. It was not until the 1960s that some sea otters from Alaska were brought to Vancouver Island to start a new colony. Now hundreds of them once again occupy the coast of British Columbia. Even so, they are still considered to be an **endangered species**.

where they feed on sea urchins, shellfish, and starfish. Mother otters float on their backs and carry their babies on their stomachs, like a raft.

Sea otters have very thick fur, which they need to keep warm and to float in the water. It was this fur that was so valuable to traders. During the period from 1790 to 1820, it was the most costly fur in the world. It was worth about ten times more than beaver fur. It was so valuable that Russian traders called the sea otter "soft gold."

Bartering for Goods

The early fur trade was a system of **barter**. Aboriginal peoples on the coast hunted for furs. Then they traded them with the sailors who came from Europe, Spain, Russia, and the United States.

When you go to a store to buy something, you pay for it with money. This is not how the fur trade worked. If the traders had offered money for furs, the Aboriginal peoples might have laughed. What use was money to them? They had nowhere to spend it. They were used to exchanging things among themselves.

Perhaps you do this with your friends. Maybe you have an apple for lunch, while your friend has a peanut butter sandwich. "Let's trade," you say. This is how the

Aboriginal peoples exchanged things. One group might have had some salmon or some baskets that another group wanted. The other group might have had some wooden tools or some berries. They got what they needed by exchanging with each other.

Making a Deal

When European traders arrived, they got used to this way of doing business. They offered kettles, blankets, knives, and other goods. Aboriginal peoples wanted these items because they were stronger and lasted longer than the goods they made for themselves out of stone and wood. In return, they offered furs and sometimes food.

When people barter, they arrive at a price by bargaining. A hunter would offer furs for a certain price, perhaps a gun. A trader would suggest that was too much and offer a blanket instead. After bargaining back and forth in this way, the hunter and the trader usually agreed on a price.

An important factor in bargaining was competition. If only one trader was working in an area, hunters had little choice in their business dealings, so the trader could make a good deal. But when more than one trader was active, trappers could offer their furs to the trader who was offering the best price.

An **endangered species** is a type of animal that is in danger of dying out completely. Endangered species are protected by law.

Think For Yourself

Here is a list of some of the goods bartered by the traders for furs:

- guns
- blankets
- knives
- tobacco
- kettles
- copper bracelets

Think about the reasons you buy the things that you do. Some things you need for your comfort. Other things make your life easier. Still other things you want just because they're fun.

Why do you think that Aboriginal peoples wanted each of the things in this list? What did each item replace that Aboriginal peoples used to make for themselves? Put your ideas in a chart like the one below

Trade Item	Used for	Replaced
guns	*hunting*	*spear*

This drawing shows a European trader and an Aboriginal hunter exchanging goods by barter.

The Fur Trade Post

Once the sea otter disappeared, traders paid more attention to the trade in beaver furs. This trade was carried on at forts that the traders built throughout the interior. Aboriginal hunters brought their furs to the posts during the year to exchange them for goods.

In the spring, when the ice melted and the rivers opened, the traders gathered up the furs and shipped them out of the country by canoe and horseback. This annual trek was called the **brigade** [bruh-GADE]. The map below shows the routes followed by the traders as they carried the furs down to the coast to be shipped back to Europe. Many of these routes were along paths used by Aboriginal peoples long before Europeans arrived. The map also shows the location of the most important fur trade posts in British Columbia.

The traders had a name for the interior of British Columbia. They called it New Caledonia [ka-luh-DOE-nee-uh], meaning New Scotland. The rolling hills and lush forests reminded them of the highlands of Scotland, the home country of some of the traders.

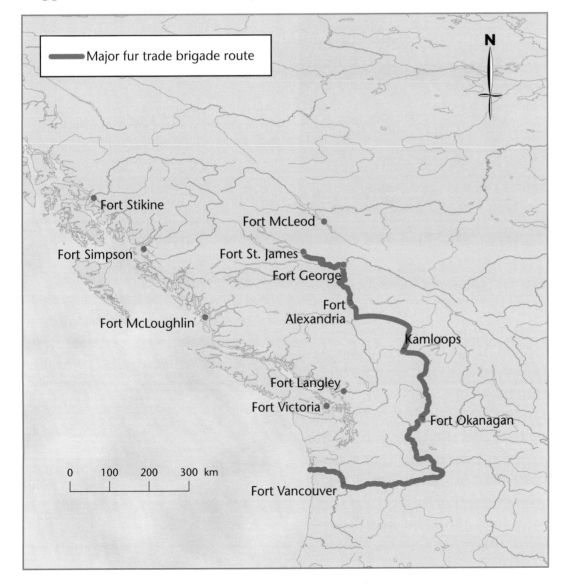

Fur trade posts were always located on water. What do you think were the reasons?

Amelia Connolly was a "daughter of the fur trade." Her mother was a Cree woman from Manitoba, and her father was an Irish trader, so Amelia herself was Métis. She grew up at trading posts all over Canada. At Fort St. James, she met a young trader named James Douglas, and they married. Later they moved to Fort Victoria, where James Douglas became the most powerful official in British Columbia. They had many children, and Amelia delighted in telling them stories about her First Nations background.

The *Beaver* was the first steamboat on the Pacific Coast. It arrived in 1836 from England. This painting shows it anchored at Fort Victoria. The traders used the *Beaver* to carry supplies to and from the posts along the coast. What advantages did steam-powered vessels have over canoes in the fur trade?

The Fur Trade Capital

Fort St. James was built in 1806 by a party of traders led by the explorer Simon Fraser. It was located in the territory of the Dakelh [dah-KELH] people, on the shores of Lake Stuart. Salmon was plentiful to feed the traders, and the Dakelh brought in a rich haul of furs. For several years, Fort St. James was considered the "capital" of the fur trade country in British Columbia.

Fort St. James belonged to the North West Company. It was one of the large companies, based in Montreal, that financed the fur trade. The other was the Hudson's Bay Company, based in London, England. For many years the two companies were rivals. In 1821 they merged, and the new Hudson's Bay Company controlled the trade from then on.

Life at Fort St. James was difficult. The climate was harsh, and there was a lot of work to do just to survive. The Dakelh brought in salmon. The traders tried to grow some of their own food, but not much grew so far north. Everything else they brought in from elsewhere by canoe brigade.

Once the fur trade was over, Fort St. James remained a small community. It was far away from any centres of population. There was nothing there to attract settlers. No road or railway came for many years.

Today Fort St. James is a community of about 2000 people. The Dakelh still live nearby. Logging is now the most important activity. The old fort has been reopened as a historic site where you can relive the exciting days of the fur trade.

Fort St. James is one of the oldest communities in British Columbia. It has been rebuilt as a historic park. How do historic sites help you learn more about life in British Columbia? Think about why it's important to preserve buildings from the past.

HOW TO... Give a Speech

Being able to speak in front of a group is an important skill. It can be a little frightening the first time you try. The best way to deal with your nerves is to be as prepared as possible and know what you're going to say. Here are some suggestions for preparing a speech:

1. Make sure that you understand your topic. Prepare some notes to guide your presentation. Highlight the main idea or ideas that you want to present.

2. Support your main idea(s) with some facts and examples.

3. Practise your speech in front of a mirror until you feel confident doing it.

4. When you give your speech, show some enthusiasm! Don't rush. Look at your audience while you're talking.

5. Finish by reminding your audience about your main idea(s). Then ask if there are any questions.

This drawing of the interior of a coastal longhouse was made by John Webber, an artist who came with the first European explorers.

Try This

When European traders first arrived, the Aboriginal peoples may have asked themselves: Should we welcome these people or should we drive them off?

Prepare a speech that an Aboriginal leader might have given to his or her people. You can try to convince them to make friends with the newcomers. Or you can try to convince them to drive the newcomers away.

Be sure to present your reasons clearly. Think carefully about what advantages contact with outsiders would bring to Aboriginal peoples. Then consider any disadvantages.

Role-play your speeches in class.

The Gold Rush

A man in tattered clothes looked up from the sandbar in the Fraser River. "We've struck it rich!" he shouted to his partner on the bank. "Gold! We've found gold!"

Later that year, 1857, a ship carried American **prospectors**, and the gold they had found, south to San Francisco. It didn't take long for people there to hear that gold had been discovered in British Columbia. Many prospectors had come to California ten years earlier to take part in the gold rush there. Now many of them rushed north to look for gold on the Fraser River.

The fur trade had not brought many newcomers to British Columbia. Only a few people were needed to operate the trading posts. The gold rush was different. When it began in 1858, about 30 000 prospectors flooded into British Columbia from the United States, Europe, China, and the rest of Canada. Some came in search of gold. Others came to set up businesses, hotels, ranches, and farms.

The gold seekers were called **prospectors** because they were looking forward to finding gold.

The artist William Hind came to British Columbia from Ontario in 1862. He had heard about the gold strikes and wanted to get a taste of adventure himself. This is one of the paintings he made when he arrived. It shows a prospector panning for gold. Gold nuggets were mixed up with gravel on the river bottom. The prospector scooped up a panful of gravel and water and swished it around. Since the gold was heavier, it stayed in the pan while the rest of the material washed out. This is how most of the early prospectors found their gold.

The **Cariboo** [KAIR-uh-boo] is an area in the interior of British Columbia. The name comes from the caribou found in the forests there.

You can find out more about the gold rush in the Cariboo by visiting the BC Archives Amazing Time Machine on the Internet. The Web site is www.bcarchives.gov.bc.ca. Click on "Time Machine."

The Impact on the Aboriginal Peoples

The Aboriginal peoples who lived along the Fraser River were concerned about the sudden influx of prospectors. What if the gold digging harmed the salmon in the river? They considered the river to be their territory. What right did the newcomers have to claim the resources? Also, the prospectors didn't always respect the customs of the Aboriginal peoples.

For a time, it looked like war might break out. But in the end, the Aboriginal peoples accepted the newcomers and agreed to share the river with them.

Travelling to the Gold Fields

The first miners travelled on trails used for many years by the Aboriginal peoples. Before long, the government began to build roads from the coast to the interior so that prospectors could travel by horseback, stagecoach, and wagon. Even so, the roads were little better than dirt tracks. Sometimes they clung to the sides of steep canyons. One false step and a horse and wagon might plunge over the cliff.

Towns sprang into existence along the roads. The most famous of the gold rush towns was Barkerville in the **Cariboo**. At its busiest, the Barkerville area had 10 000 residents. For a while, it was the largest town north of San Francisco. In just ten years, about $26 million worth of gold was taken out of the mines and creeks around Barkerville.

In time, the gold began to run out. As the nuggets disappeared from the creeks, miners had to dig deeper into the ground. They had to use explosives and more expensive ways of bringing the gold to the surface. Only companies with a lot of money could take part in this next stage of mining. The prospectors began to drift away. By 1874, just ten years after the Cariboo's busiest and richest year, only a few hundred people remained in Barkerville.

The gold rush was over.

A Closer Look

The Cariboo Road

The Cariboo Road was built by soldiers brought to British Columbia from England. It was a dirt road, built for horse-drawn wagons. It ran for 164 kilometres, from Yale on the Fraser River to Barkerville in the Cariboo.

It was an incredible feat of construction. Along the steep-sided canyons, the road sometimes seemed to hang in the air. All sorts of traffic travelled along it, from pack mules to speedy stagecoaches. Even camels were used for a while.

The Cariboo Road was a toll road. This meant that travellers had to pay a fee to use it. The money was used to make improvements to the road.

Much of the route of the Cariboo Road is now part of the modern highway system in British Columbia.

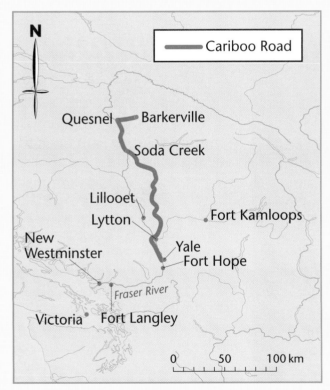

N

Cariboo Road

Quesnel — Barkerville
Soda Creek
Lillooet
Lytton
Fort Kamloops
New Westminster
Yale
Fort Hope
Fraser River
Victoria Fort Langley

0   50   100 km

This map shows the route of the Cariboo Road. What river did the road follow? Why do you think the builders preferred to keep close to the river?

This scene shows people travelling on the Cariboo Road, high above the Fraser River. One traveller described it like this: "No fence whatever, and certain death to fall over the precipice into the river." Why do you think it was so important to build a road to the gold fields?

REAL PEOPLE: BILLY BARKER (1817–1894)

The most famous prospector of all was Billy Barker. He was so famous they named a town after him—Barkerville. You can still visit Barkerville, which has been rebuilt to look just like it did 100 years ago.

Billy was an Englishman who left his home as a young man to seek gold in North America. And find gold he did! His strike on Williams Creek started a mad rush of prospectors into the Cariboo district of British Columbia. The mine that he located produced 1.3 tonnes of gold before it was closed.

By that time, Billy had sold his share of the mine to someone else. He took his money and lived a life of leisure for a while. But pretty soon all the money was gone, and Billy ended up living in poverty.

The problem for the miners was separating pieces of gold from dirt and gravel. This photograph shows one of the solutions. It was called a **rocker**. One miner shovelled dirt into the top of the box where it was mixed with water. Another miner used the handle to shake, or rock, the box in order to separate out the gold. The water carried the rest of the debris (fragments left behind) out the bottom. Why was this technique better than panning?

In The Words Of...

An Eye Witness

Here is what one eye-witness wrote about the gold rush:

Ocean steamers from California, crowded with gold-seekers, arrived every two or three days in Victoria. This place, previously a quiet hamlet, containing two or three hundred people, was suddenly converted into a scene of bustle and excitement. In the brief space of four months, 20 000 souls poured into the harbour. The sound of hammer and axe was heard in every direction. Shops, stores and shanties to the number of 225 arose in six weeks.

Excerpt from the Reverend Matthew Macfie, *Vancouver Island and British Columbia*, London, 1865.

A New Beginning

The gold rush marked the beginning of settlement in British Columbia. Many miners moved away when the rush was over. But many people stayed, making lives for themselves in the communities and on the farms.

As a result of the arrival of the miners, British Columbia was given a government in 1858. The Cariboo Road and other roads built for the gold rush provided a network of transportation. Many businesses and farms got their start during the gold rush, then remained in operation after it was over.

In all these ways, the gold rush marked a turning point for British Columbia.

Think For Yourself

As you saw in the account above, Victoria grew rapidly during the gold rush. Even when the rush was over, Victoria continued to grow. On the other hand, towns like Barkerville became ghost towns. Everyone moved away.

Can you explain why this happens? Why do certain towns "boom" and then go "bust"? Why do other communities survive and prosper? Discuss your ideas in small groups.

Try This

Imagine that you are living in Barkerville in 1863. You look ahead and see that the gold rush will soon end. You are worried about the future of your community. Think about what the community could do to make sure that it doesn't disappear.

In a group, draw up a plan to present to the town council. You'll have to analyze the problems facing the community, then find solutions to these problems. Brainstorm some ideas for activities that will help the community survive. What about possibilities for attracting tourists to the area? This is just one idea. Your group will have many more. Use a flow chart like this one to organize your planning.

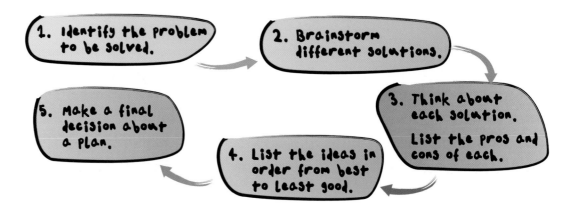

1. Identify the problem to be solved.

2. Brainstorm different solutions.

3. Think about each solution. List the pros and cons of each.

4. List the ideas in order from best to least good.

5. Make a final decision about a plan.

Present your plan to the rest of the class, who can role-play the town council. Part of your presentation might include a survey that asks residents for their ideas.

Looking Back

In this chapter, you learned about some of the natural resources that have made Canada such a rich country. Two important resources in British Columbia, furs and gold, led to the development of the province.

What does the study of natural resources help us to understand about Canada?

THE SALMON CANNERIES

Chapter **10**

Have you ever walked down the street and seen a picture of a fish painted on the pavement? You probably have if you live near a river or close to the ocean.

The pictures are usually painted close to a street drain. They are a new kind of warning sign. They are saying, "Don't dump anything down this drain that will harm the fish!" They remind people that water flowing into the drains will end up in the streams and rivers where salmon live. If poison chemicals get into the water, the salmon might be killed.

In the last chapter, you learned about some of British Columbia's natural resources. Salmon are another resource— a very important one.

In this chapter, you can learn about the role played by the salmon in the life of British Columbia. As you work through the chapter, think about ways of making sure that the salmon do not disappear.

RIVER OF SALMON

The Adams River is a short, rushing river in the interior of British Columbia. Once every four years, in October, it is the site of one of the most amazing natural events in the world: the return of the sockeye salmon.

Millions of salmon return to the river from the sea to **spawn**, or lay eggs. Their skin has turned bright red so that the river runs like blood. There are so many fish that you could almost walk across the river on their backs.

This map shows the route followed by the sockeye that swim from the Adams River to the Pacific. What is the name of the major river they follow? The Adams River is one of many rivers in British Columbia where the salmon spawn. Find out if there is a river near you where you can see the salmon return in the autumn.

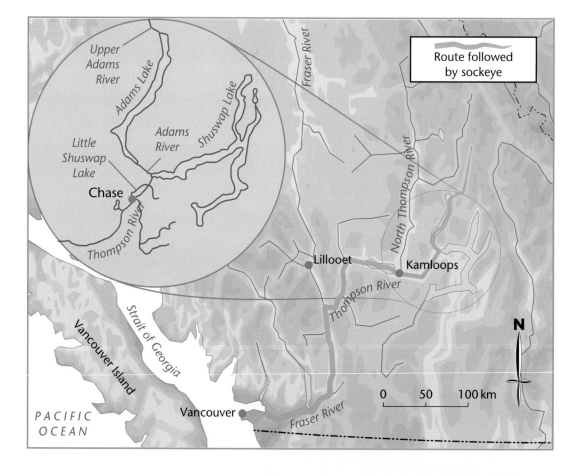

Route followed by sockeye

REAL PEOPLE: RODERICK HAIG-BROWN (1908–1976)

Roderick Haig-Brown lived in Campbell River, a city on Vancouver Island that is famous for its salmon fishing. He was an avid fisher, and when he wasn't fishing himself he was writing about it.

Haig-Brown wrote many books for readers of all ages. He wrote about other animals, but his books about fish and fishing are considered his best. One of his children's books, *Saltwater Summer*, received a Governor General's Award. He tried to awaken in his readers a respect for the fish and a love of wild nature.

During his lifetime, Roderick Haig-Brown led many fights to save wild rivers from changes that would ruin them. He worried that dams and industries would make it impossible for the salmon to use the rivers.

The sockeye lay their eggs on the gravel bottom of the river. Then, their journey complete, they die. Slowly their bodies rot in the water, turning into food that the young fish will feed on when they are born. In this way, the cycle of nature is complete.

This stretch of the Adams River is protected as a provincial park so that everyone can marvel at the return of the salmon. The park is named for the writer and fly fisher Roderick Haig-Brown.

Here's the Salmon!

Salmon are fascinating fish. They are born in fresh water, many kilometres from the ocean. Once they've spent some time fattening up, they swim downstream to the ocean where they live most of their lives in salt water. After several years, when they're ready to spawn, salmon return to the stream in which they were born. There they lay their eggs and then they die.

How do salmon find their way home? It has something to do with the smell of the water, the light patterns, and perhaps **magnetism**. No one knows for sure. What we do know is that salmon will swim thousands of kilometres to get to the exact spot where they were born.

Magnetism [MAG-ne-tiz-im] is a natural force through which objects are attracted to each other.

One type of salmon doesn't migrate to the ocean. It spends its whole life in freshwater lakes and streams. It is called the kokanee.

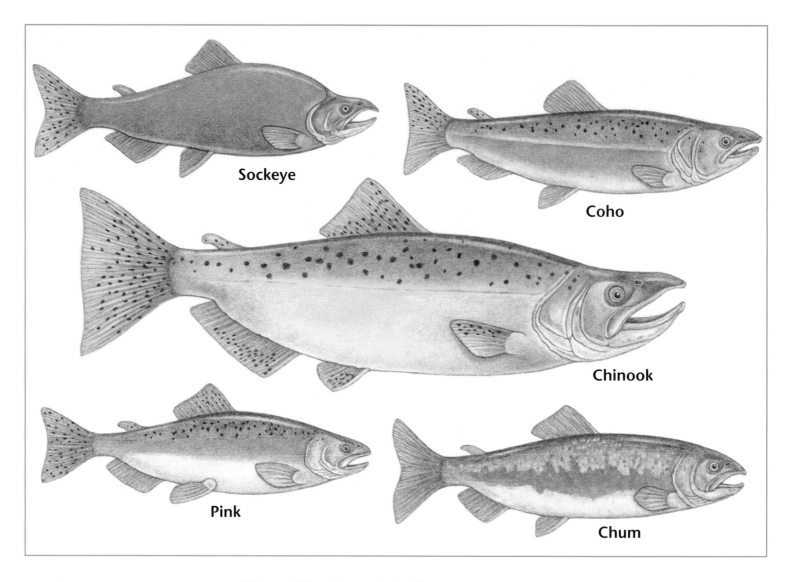

Sockeye

Coho

Chinook

Pink

Chum

What physical differences would you use to tell one type of salmon from another?

Five Kinds of Salmon

British Columbia has five types of salmon. There are slight differences in appearance and life habits between each type.

Sockeye [SOK-eye] are the tastiest. As British Columbia became world famous for its salmon, it was sockeye that won this reputation.

Coho [KOE-hoe] put up a good fight when they are hooked. They are the most popular with sport fishers.

Chinook [shih-NOOK] grow to be the biggest. When they reach 13.5 kilograms, they are known as tyees, a real trophy for sport fishers!

Pink are the most numerous type of salmon, and the smallest. As males grow bigger, they develop a hump, so they are sometimes called humpbacks.

Chum are not liked much by consumers. This type used to be caught for dog food so it earned the name "dog salmon."

A Closer Look

Fish Hatcheries

If you are learning about salmon, there's no better way than to see them than in real life. There are a lot of places where you can do this, without even getting your feet wet. One place is a fish hatchery. There are many fish hatcheries on rivers around British Columbia.

One hatchery that is open to visitors is on the Capilano River in North Vancouver. Years ago, a dam was built on the Capilano River to create a reservoir to supply Vancouver with water. The dam made it impossible for salmon to reach their spawning places. They couldn't get past the huge wall of concrete now blocking the river. Salmon began to die off in the river.

The hatchery was built as an answer to this problem. Fish are raised to a young age in large tanks. They are fed a healthy diet and protected from other animals that feed on them in the wild. When they reach a certain size, they are released into the river. From there they swim to the ocean.

Find Out

Find out if there is a hatchery near your community that your class could visit.

If you're not able to visit a hatchery in person, you can visit one on the Internet. Several hatcheries in BC, including the one on the Capilano River, have Web sites. You can find them through Fisheries and Oceans Canada at:

www-heb.pac.dfo-mpo.gc.ca/english/facilities/Capilano/capilano.htm.

Before your visit, take some time to do a Know-Wonder-Learn exercise. Make a chart with three columns. In the first column, write down what you already know about fish hatcheries. In the second column, write down what you'd like to know—what you wonder about hatcheries.

During your visit, ask questions and make notes. When you're back in class, fill in the last column of your chart. What did you learn during your visit? Were all your "Wonder" questions answered?

Fish Hatcheries		
KNOW	WONDER	LEARN

CATCHING AND CANNING

When fish are being caught in order to be sold to other people, we call it **commercial fishing**. When fish are being caught by people who are just out having fun, we call it **sport fishing**. Many sport fishers don't even keep the salmon they catch. They release them back into the water. This is called **catch and release**. It helps to make sure that the salmon will survive.

Gang knives were several blades mounted on one device and operated by a single worker.

Fishers catch many types of fish in the waters off the coast of British Columbia. These include halibut, cod, and herring. But no fish is more important than the salmon.

Aboriginal peoples relied on salmon as a food supply. They ate the fish fresh out of the water. They also preserved it by drying it in the sun and smoking it over fires. In this way, the salmon lasted all year.

When Europeans arrived in British Columbia, they began catching salmon in order to sell them to customers in other countries. Once a salmon is caught, it doesn't stay fresh for very long. Nowadays we simply freeze it to keep it fresh. But in the early days of commercial fishing, there was no freezing. Instead, fish were packed in barrels in a salt brine to keep them from rotting.

Then, around 1870, canning came into use as a new way of preserving the salmon. Canned fish will last a long time without going bad. Canning led to the development of a flourishing new industry in British Columbia.

Fish Factories

The first salmon cannery in British Columbia opened near the mouth of the Fraser River in 1867. From there the industry expanded northward up the coast. By the 1920s, there were dozens of canneries. They were located at the mouths of all the major rivers and up the ocean inlets.

Canneries were large factories built at the water's edge. They only operated during the summer, when the salmon were swimming into the rivers on their way to spawn. This is when fishers went out in their boats to catch them in huge numbers.

After the fishers filled their boats, they brought their catches to the cannery dock. The salmon were unloaded and hauled to long tables, where they were cut up and cleaned. The razor-sharp knives flashed as the butchers did their work.

Elsewhere in the cannery, other crews were cutting up sheets of tin and shaping them into cans. When each can was filled with fish, it was sealed shut and boiled in a tank to cook it. Labels were glued to the cans, which were packed in cases for shipping to customers all over the world.

It was a noisy, steamy, smelly atmosphere, where people were on their feet working for ten hours a day.

Machines and Fish

Canning was a job that was always changing as new machines were invented. Steam cookers speeded up the cooking. **Gang knives** cut up several fish at once. Other machines cut up the tin so that it no longer had to be done by hand. Finally, an automatic can-making machine was introduced that did the whole job itself.

One of the most important machines was the Smith Butchering Machine. It was named for its inventor, E. A. Smith. This machine was able to cut up 75 salmon every minute. It did the work of 20 workers.

The result of all these machines was to speed up the canning process. Each new machine made the process faster. It also replaced the workers who had done the job before.

These are two young women who worked in a cannery. Many of the workers in the canneries were women. Almost all the fishers were men. Why do you think women did certain jobs and men did others?

Cans of salmon were decorated with colourful labels. Notice the images that the canners used on the labels. Why do you think they chose these images?

Cannery Villages

The canneries were like small cities. Workers came with their families to stay for the summer. They lived in tents and boarding houses behind the cannery. Every member of the family worked at a job. Even the children did simple chores.

People from many different backgrounds worked at the salmon canneries. Many of the fishers who supplied the salmon were Japanese or Aboriginal men. Inside the cannery, Chinese men and Aboriginal women did the work.

When the season ended and the cannery closed, the Aboriginal families moved back to their villages for the winter. The other workers drifted away to find different jobs on farms or in sawmills, lumber camps, and mines.

Find Out

Are there jobs today that only women do and other jobs that only men do? You can do your own study of this question. For an entire week, keep a list called "Who Does What?" When you see a job being done, include it in your list and note whether it's being done by a man or a woman. By the end of the week, you should have a wide selection of jobs: librarian, teacher, store clerk, dentist, bus driver, and so on.

Sort your findings in a Venn diagram like this one.

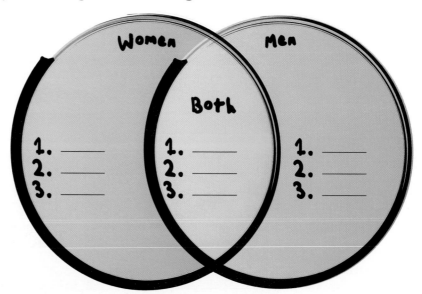

Do men and women do different work? Discuss your results in class.

This photograph shows the North Pacific Cannery Village. It is located near the mouth of the Skeena River in northern British Columbia. It was a working cannery from 1889 to 1972. About 700 people worked here during the summer season. Today, it is a historic site where you can go to see what life was like for the people who worked at a salmon cannery.

Think For Yourself

Changes are happening all the time in the way things are made. New machinery is invented. New ways of doing things are introduced. All industries are affected.

Think about this process of change in the case of the salmon canning industry. What benefits did the use of new machinery bring to the owners of the canneries? What benefits did the workers receive? Were there any disadvantages of the new machinery? Use a chart like this one to organize your findings.

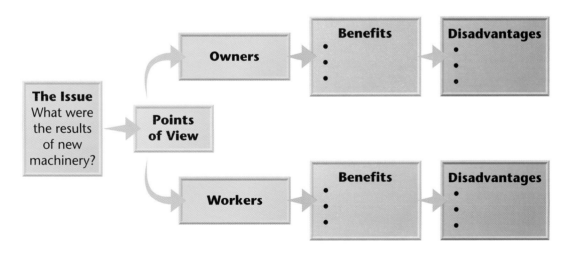

Who would you say benefited the most from the changes? How did they benefit?

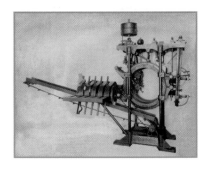

In 1905, the salmon canneries were faced with a shortage of workers. The Smith Butchering Machine was introduced in 1906 to reduce this problem.

Find Out

Make a study of change in another industry—one that is important to your community. It could be a sawmill or the computer industry. Invite someone who works in the industry to visit your class to talk about the changes that have gone on in the past 10 or 20 years.

Take notes as your guest speaks. Sort the information into categories:

- *Why were the changes made?*

- *How have they benefited the industry and the people who work in it?*

- *How have they affected your community?*

After the visit, identify one or two main ideas that you think are most important.

A **key word** can be a name, a word from one of your questions, or a word that is connected to the main idea.

Taking notes is an important part of doing research and of listening. You can't remember everything you read or hear. Notes allow you to keep track of the main ideas and facts that you might not remember.

1. Write down two or three basic questions that you want to answer.

2. List the **key words** that might help you find the information you need. When you see or hear these key words, you'll know that you need to record this information.

3. Write down only the main ideas.

4. Write as clearly as possible. You want to be able to read your notes later!

FISHING FOR A LIVING

For as long as anyone can remember, salmon have been plentiful in the oceans off British Columbia. Fishers have had no trouble making a living. Many small communities along the coast have depended on this resource for their survival.

Recently, the situation seems to have changed. The salmon are no longer returning to the coast in huge numbers. Some people blame the fishers for catching too many. Other people say the rivers are polluted, so the fish are dying off. Still others say the ocean is getting warmer, causing the salmon to change their habits.

Whatever the reasons are, there is no doubt that we're going to have to be more careful about conserving the salmon. A similar situation occurred on the east coast of Canada. There the people relied on the cod fish, which they sold to customers all over the world. For hundreds of years, the cod fishery supported communities in Newfoundland and the other Atlantic provinces. Then the cod disappeared. Too many fishers—from Canada and from other countries—caught too many fish. Cod fishers on the Atlantic coast had to tie up their boats. The communities dwindled.

In British Columbia, no one wants the same thing to happen to the salmon fishery. People in the province are trying to agree on what to do about it.

This scene shows a trawler in Johnstone Strait, British Columbia.

In The Words Of...

A Fishing Community

Here's what different members of a fishing community might say about conserving the salmon fishery.

A commercial fisher

My father was a fisher, and I am a fisher. I own a very expensive boat and lots of equipment. I need to fish to support my family. I have no other way of making a living. Fishing is all I know and, anyway, it's the only work in this town. There are enough people looking for work already, without throwing all the fishers out of work. Sure, we need to conserve the salmon. But it's important to allow small fishers like me to catch enough fish to survive.

The mayor

Half our town is supported by fishing. Fishers spend their money at the stores in town. People repair boats and engines. If there was no fishing industry, many people would be out of work. They wouldn't be able to find jobs so they would have to leave town. Our town would die. And lots of sport fishers come here to catch salmon. They spend a lot of money here. If there are no fish for them, that will be a big problem.

A sport fisher

I love to fish. I come here every year, and I go home with a few salmon. I'm happy to spend a lot of money here. It's my vacation. If I couldn't catch fish, I wouldn't come back. I understand the need to conserve fish. But I think the government should still allow each of us to catch a few fish.

An environmentalist

It's no good arguing about how many fish each person can catch. If we keep on arguing and keep on catching fish, there will be no fish left to argue about. We need to stop all fishing until the salmon have had a chance to recover. I know that people will be hurt. So will communities. And that is unfortunate. But we have to put the fish first. If we don't, they'll disappear and there will be no fishing anyway—ever.

A First Nations leader

We've fished this coast for thousands of years, and there was always enough fish for everyone. We have a right to keep on fishing for food, as we have done for hundreds of generations. We are willing to share the industry. We always have. But it's only right that we get our share.

Look at Different Points of View

People have different ideas about almost everything. These ideas are called points of view. It's important to be able to look at a subject from someone else's point of view. You don't have to agree with the other person, but try to understand his or her reasons.

1. Pay attention to other points of view. Don't refuse to hear them. Think about what they mean.

2. Remember that everyone has good ideas.

3. What is the main idea of someone else's point of view? Is there part of it that you agree with?

4. Are you willing to change your own point of view if someone else has good ideas?

Think For Yourself

Each member of the fishing community agrees there is a problem. The problem is a lack of fish. The problem has different **causes**, and for each speaker it has different **effects**. (The cause is the person or thing that makes something happen. The effect is a change produced by a cause.)

Identify the effects and organize them in a cause-and-effect chart like the one shown here.

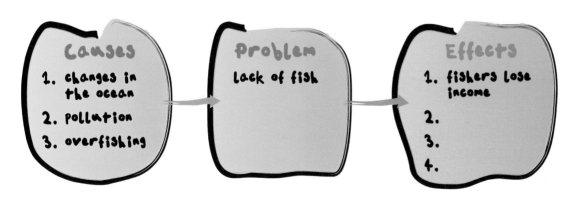

Causes
1. changes in the ocean
2. pollution
3. overfishing

Problem
lack of fish

Effects
1. fishers lose income
2.
3.
4.

"Our culture, our spirituality, our very existence is directly tied to the salmon. Here, on the Nass River, the Nisga'a have been fishing for thousands of years. We always share the salmon with our neighbours, whether they are Aboriginal or non-Aboriginal. But we also insist on catching our own share, as it says in our historic treaty."

—Harry Nyce, a Nisga'a fisher

Find Out

Remember those fish that are painted on the street? A lot of that painting was done by young people like yourselves. They decided that they wanted to help conserve the salmon, so they got involved. You can get involved as well.

First of all, do some research to find out as much as you can about the salmon and its habitat. Then use your knowledge to inform other people. Contact your local government to share your concerns and to find out what is being done to conserve the salmon.

Perhaps you can paint signs on the drains in your community. Or you could organize a cleanup of a stream where salmon used to spawn. Or you could design a poster with a "Save the Salmon" message. These are all ways that you can make a difference.

Looking Back

Salmon has been an important resource in British Columbia for many years. In this chapter, you thought about how the salmon could be conserved, along with the communities that depend on it.

Why do you think it is important to protect our natural resources?

Chapter 11

Building Our Communities

People have lived together in communities in Canada for generations.

Long ago, these communities were small, just a family or two. Everyone knew each other. Today, many of our communities have grown very large. They are full of people from many diverse backgrounds doing many diverse activities.

In this chapter, you can learn about cities and some of the problems they are facing. You can also think about ways that people can make communities better places in which to live.

You are part of this challenge. Explore ways that you can help to improve your own community.

Starting a Revolution

We hear the world *revolution* used a lot these days. Usually it refers to politics. When one group overthrows another by force and seizes control of the government, we say there has been a revolution.

Really, though, revolution can refer to any sudden change in the world that affects the lives of many people. A few years ago, when everyone started using computers, it was called the computer revolution. When we change the style of clothes we wear, we call it a fashion revolution. Today, people say that we are living through an information revolution. This means that we have access to much more information than ever before.

The Industrial Revolution

One of the greatest periods of change in human history was the **Industrial Revolution**. It took place in many countries around the world. The Industrial Revolution began in Great Britain around 1760, then spread to the rest of Europe and North America. In Canada, it took place near the end of the 1800s.

These were some of the important changes that took place during the Industrial Revolution:

This painting, by William Armstrong, shows an early factory in Toronto in 1864. Imagine working in such a place. How do you think the workers feel about their jobs?

- New materials were used to make goods. Iron and steel replaced wood and stone.

- New sources of energy were discovered. Steam replaced muscle, wind, and water as the source of power.

- New machines were invented. Railways and steamships made transportation faster. In the factory, machines like the spinning jenny increased the speed of work.

If you lived in Canada at that time, you would have seen the Industrial Revolution going on all around you. Here are just some of the changes:

- Electric lights took the place of candles and oil lamps.

- Telephones became a part of many homes.

- Streetcars and railways replaced the horse and buggy.

- Large factories took the place of small workshops.

- Machines of all types replaced animals as a source of labour.

The photograph on the left shows a shoemaker in his workshop. The photograph on the right shows women at work in a factory. Use these two photographs to describe the changes in the workplace brought about by the Industrial Revolution. What do you see? What words would you use to describe each work situation?

These young boys worked in a Montreal factory in the early 1900s.

The Great Change

The greatest change that occurred during the Industrial Revolution was the change in the way things were made. The process by which raw materials are used to make other goods is called **manufacturing**.

Before the Industrial Revolution, Canada was a producer of natural resources like fur, fish, timber, and minerals. During the Industrial Revolution, the big change that occurred in Canada was that the country began using its resources to manufacture many more goods.

Manufacturing led to many new jobs and to new opportunities for business people. Factories were built. The power of machines was put to work. Railways stretched across the country. The lives of Canadians changed forever.

Machines and Factories

In the last chapter, you learned how machines changed the salmon cannery. You saw how one new machine might produce more goods and replace many workers. The canneries are just one example. The same thing was happening in every industry at the same time.

Before the Industrial Revolution, most goods were made by hand. The dressmaker sewed a dress. The shoemaker cut leather and stitched a boot. The coal miner laboured with pick and shovel. There weren't many machines to help them.

Machines made work easier and faster. A steam engine powering a hammer or a sewing machine could make many more goods than someone working by hand. The spinning jenny wound fibres around a spindle so that one spinner could make much more cloth. These were just a few of many inventions.

Steam engines operated many machines at the same time. These machines, and the people who ran them, were brought together in one building, called a factory. Factories became the new workplace of the Industrial Revolution.

A Closer Look

Children at Work

In the early days of the Industrial Revolution, most children worked either at home or at a job. Families needed the extra money. School was considered less important.

Théophile Charron [tay-oe-FEEL sha-RO(N)] was a 14-year-old boy who lived in Montreal in 1886. He worked in a factory making cigars. He began as an apprentice, someone who learns on the job. Here are answers he gave to some questions about his work:

Question: *You began working at 11 years?*

Answer: *Yes.*

Question: *What wages did you get during your apprenticeship?*

Answer: *One dollar a week for the first year, $1.50 for the second year, and $2 for the third year. When I worked extra I got more.*

Question: *Did you have any fines to pay during your apprenticeship?*

Answer: *Yes.*

Question: *Many?*

Answer: *A good number.*

Question: *How many hours did you work a day?*

Answer: *Sometimes ten hours, other times eight hours. It was just as they wanted it.*

Question: *Do you remember why you paid these fines?*

Answer: *Sometimes for talking too much; mostly for that.*

Question: *You were never licked?*

Answer: *Yes; not licked so as any harm was done me, but sometimes they would come along, and if we happened to be cutting tobacco wrong, they would give us a crack across the head with the fist.*

Question: *Was it usual to beat children like that?*

Answer: *Yes.*

From testimony at the Royal Commission on the Relations of Labour and Capital.

Think For Yourself

Do you know of any jobs that 14-year-olds are allowed to do today? Make a list of them.

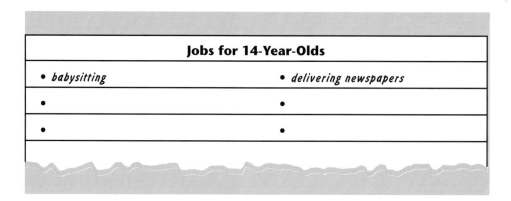

Jobs for 14-Year-Olds	
• *babysitting*	• *delivering newspapers*
•	•
•	•

Discuss the reasons why young people are no longer allowed to work at most jobs.

Try This

Think about the differences between your life and the life of a child like Théophile working in a factory.

Compare your life to Théophile's. Do you have any jobs to do? What do you do in your spare time? What do you hope to do when you have finished school?

You may want to use a comparison chart like the one shown here. Can you think of other differences to add to the chart?

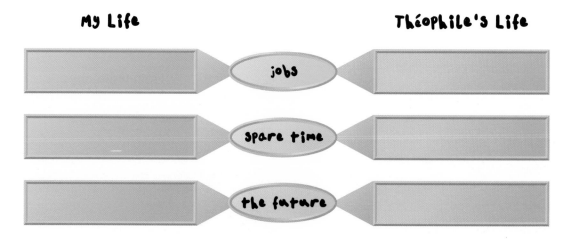

Good and Bad

The Industrial Revolution led to rapid economic growth. Canada became a manufacturing nation. The way people lived also changed. Railways, electric lights, telephones, washing machines, and automobiles—these were all among the new goods that were being manufactured.

At the same time, for many people the Industrial Revolution brought poverty and misery. Factories were not pleasant places in which to work. They were noisy, dirty, and unhealthy. Workers had to labour for long hours at the new machines.

By today's standards, the lives of working people were hard. They were on the job for ten or twelve hours a day, six days a week. There was little time for relaxation or family. When jobs were lost, there was no insurance or sick pay. Workers injured on the job had to fend for themselves.

Sharing the Wealth

There was a long struggle to share the wealth created by the Industrial Revolution among all the people. As time passed, conditions in the factories got better. The lives of working people and their children improved. Many of these improvements came about because people demanded changes that made the workplace safer and healthier.

Laws were passed limiting the hours that people had to work. Safety rules were put into place. When workers lost their jobs or got sick, they received some **compensation** [kom-pun-SAY-shun].

Workers were no longer the victims of change. Instead, they were able to share the benefits of change.

Compensation is something (often money) given to a person to make up for a loss or an injury.

During the Winnipeg General Strike of 1919, over 30 000 workers demonstrated against low wages and poor working conditions.

Try This

Imagine that you have opened a time capsule that was buried by a school class like your own in 1900. The students wanted the capsule to show what life was like for them at the time. Make a list of the things they might have included.

Now compose a list for your own time capsule, recording life at the beginning of the 21st century. What will you include?

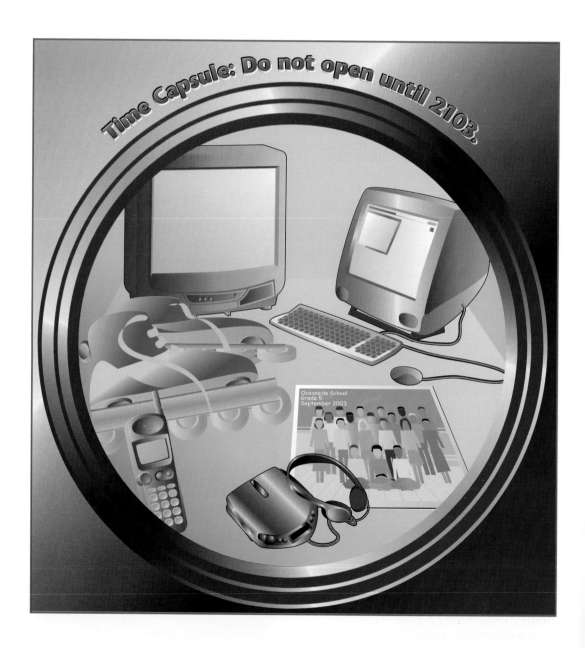

Moving from the Country to the City

Think about how many people you know who live on farms in the country. By growing crops and raising animals, these people do important work providing food for the cities. In the early days of Canada, most people lived on farms.

Now think about how many of your friends and family live in towns or cities. If you're like most people, your world is the world of the city. More than three out of every four Canadians live in an **urban area**. This means a town or a city.

Canada has become a nation of city dwellers. So how did this change come about?

The Growth of Cities

One of the biggest changes of the Industrial Revolution was the growth of cities. In the early days, communities grew up around trading posts or forts. During the Industrial Revolution, cities grew because of industry. Factories were built in a few centres where transportation was available, along with a supply of workers.

The new industrial cities were different from the towns of early Canada. Streets were paved, and houses were crowded together. There was the bustle and noise of traffic. Factories belched smoke into the air.

More and more people came to live in the cities because that was where they could find work. Canada slowly changed from being a rural society to mainly an urban society. Can you explain some of the differences between lifestyles in each of these societies?

It was during the 1920s that Canada became an urban country. For the first time, more people lived in cities than lived in the country.

A Closer Look

Vancouver: A Port City

One of the reasons Vancouver grew so rapidly was its location. Vancouver lies at the mouth of the Fraser River. Traffic coming down from the interior is funnelled by the river right past the city's doorstep.

Vancouver also has a fine harbour. As a result, it became a port city where ships from around the world load cargo.

You can visit the port yourself. The people who work there welcome tours of school children. Just be sure to arrange your visit ahead of time.

If you don't live near Vancouver, you can visit the port on the Internet. The Web site is www.portvancouver.com.

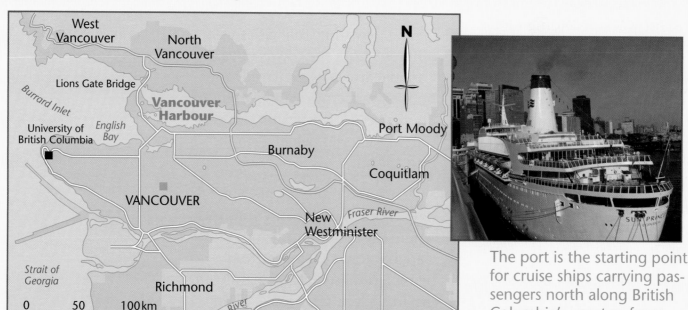

The port is the starting point for cruise ships carrying passengers north along British Columbia's coast as far as Alaska.

Some facts about the Port of Vancouver:

- In 1998, 873 102 cruise-ship passengers passed through the port.
- The port ships 70 million tonnes of cargo every year.
- Some exported products include lumber, coal, grain, sulphur, and wood pulp.
- Every year, 725 000 containers pass through the port.

Countries receiving the most cargo shipped from the port:

1. Japan
2. South Korea
3. China
4. Brazil
5. Taiwan
6. USA
7. Great Britain
8. Italy
9. Indonesia
10. Mexico

A lot of cargo is carried in huge containers that are loaded on ships by giant cranes. The containers make it easier to handle the cargo. Vancouver is the largest port in Canada.

Try This

The map, photographs, and statistics on pages 176 to 177 tell the story of the Port of Vancouver. As you look at this information, take notes under these headings to record your findings:

What products are exported through the port?	How do these products arrive at the port?
Where in British Columbia or Canada do you think these products come from?	In your atlas, locate the countries that are the best customers for goods shipped from the port.

Try This

	1891	1921	1961	1996
Vancouver	13 709	163 220	826 798	1 831 000
Toronto	181 215	521 000	1 919 409	4 236 000
Montreal	219 616	618 506	2 215 627	3 326 000
Winnipeg	25 639	179 087	476 000	667 000

This chart shows the population size for different years of four cities in Canada. For each year, rank the cities from largest to smallest.

Which city grew the most during each period? Can you think of reasons that might explain why some cities grow faster than others?

This scene shows the old part of Montreal, which attracts many tourists, especially during the summer. There are many interesting things to do like visiting historical buildings, watching the street performers, and rollerblading at the old port.

Find Out

Use your atlas to find out which of the countries receiving cargo from the port are part of the Pacific Rim.

Growing Pains

Growth never seems to occur without growing pains. You have learned that cities in Canada grew rapidly after 1900. At the same time, rapid growth brought problems, many of which are still with us today.

When you go for a drive with your family, do you find the roads choked with traffic? Are there sometimes warnings on the radio about the quality of the air? Is the water coming out of your taps ever murky in colour? These are all signs of some of the problems facing the modern city. Can you think of any others?

Urban Problems

Most of the problems facing the city are caused by two factors:

- the large number of people who live there

- the high level of industry that takes place

The variety that city life offers is what makes it so exciting. But there is a price to be paid. Three-quarters of all Canadians live in urban areas. Such a large number of people produces a lot of pollution. Cars spew gas fumes into the air. Garbage piles up and has to be stored somewhere. Sewage is pumped into the rivers and the ocean. The need for clean water grows steadily.

Cars and trucks are a major cause of air pollution.

This same situation exists around the world. At the beginning of the 20th century, only 14 per cent of all the people in the world lived in towns and cities. By the year 2005, half of all humankind will be urban dwellers.

Some of these cities will be gigantic. We call them **mega-cities**. By 2015, Bombay, a city in India, will have 27 million people. Tokyo, the capital of Japan, will have 28 million. New York, the largest city in North America, will have 17 million. How will so many people be able to live comfortably together? This is one of the great challenges facing the world as the 21st century begins.

Air Pollution

Polluted air is a serious problem for modern cities. The problem used to be much worse. When most homes were heated by coal and wood, the air was full of soot. This is the black powder that is left by the smoke. Modern fuels such as natural gas burn much more cleanly.

Modern cities face a different challenge: the automobile. Most families now own a car, sometimes two or even three. We think we need them for our busy lives. How often do you use a car every day, even when you could be walking or taking a bus?

Cars are terrible polluters. They give out fumes that dirty the air and are harmful to breathe. They use up oil that is thrown away into the environment. And when we buy new cars, the rusting hulks of our old cars pile up in the junkyard.

Smokestack industries are another main source of high pollution levels.

Think For Yourself

You often have a choice between using a car and taking **public transit**. Buses, subways, and trains are all examples of public transit.

City planners are always trying to persuade more people to ride on public transit. What are the advantages of using it? Are there disadvantages?

How would you convince people to park their cars and ride the bus? Brainstorm some ideas in your class. List them in a web diagram.

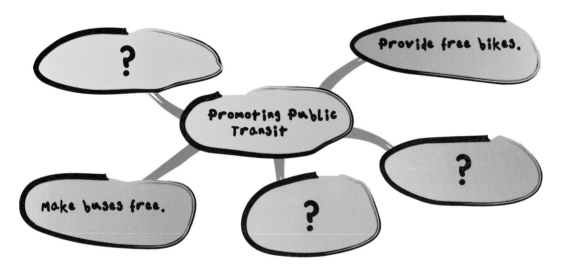

Once you have a variety of ideas, decide which are the best ones. Then invite an official from your local public transit company to visit your class. Share the ideas with your visitor and invite comments.

How can you play a role in making your community a better place?

Using Resources

Cities occupy only a small area, compared to the large tracts of forest and farmland that surround them. On the other hand, cities devour a huge share of the natural resources that are available.

Think about all the things your city needs to survive. It needs food to feed the people. It needs clean water for drinking. It needs electrical power to run the lights and machinery, gas to run the automobiles, and paper to print the newspapers.

For all these things—and many more—the city draws on the land that surrounds it. Food is brought in from farms. Electricity is produced at power dams faraway in the interior and is carried by wires to the city. Trees are cut down to make paper.

All these resources are necessary to keep a city liveable.

Try This

Here are some words that describe a liveable city:

- safe

- clean

- healthy

- environmentally friendly

- beautiful

Can you think of other words to add to the list? Next to each word, suggest one or more ways your own community could be improved to make it fit this description. For example, your community could plant public gardens to make it more beautiful.

Communities remain liveable because the people who live there help to keep them that way!

Looking Back

In this chapter, you saw how the Industrial Revolution brought great changes to Canada and to the world. One of the biggest changes was the growth of cities, which created problems that we still face today.

In your everyday life, what can you do to make your community a better place?

Chapter 12

Renewing Our World

In earlier chapters of this book, you learned about some of the natural resources in Canada and in British Columbia. These included water, coal, fish, gold, and many others.

Natural resources don't last forever. The sea otter teaches us that, as we saw in Chapter 9. During the time of the fur trade, the sea otter was hunted out of existence. In our own time, some people think the same thing might happen to the salmon if we're not careful.

In this chapter, you can learn how to protect our resources so that they will last for future generations.

Paper or Plastic?

This worker is planting new trees in an area that has been logged. Each year in Canada millions of new trees are planted. A Christmas tree takes ten years to grow. Think about how long it takes to grow a tree tall enough for logging.

When you go to the store to buy groceries, the clerk asks you, "Paper or plastic?" Do you want to carry home your purchases in plastic bags or paper ones?

You may say plastic. It seems easier to carry things in a plastic bag. Or you may choose paper, thinking you can later cut up the bag for crafts. But do you ever stop to ask yourself where the bags come from? There may be other reasons for choosing paper or plastic.

Running Out of Resources

Both paper and plastic bags are made from natural resources. Plastic bags are made from oil, or petroleum. Paper bags come from wood pulp, which is made from trees.

Oil is found in large pools underground. It is pumped to the surface, then sent to markets through long pipelines. Plastic bags are just one of many products made from oil.

There is only a limited amount of oil in the world. When we use it, it can't be replaced. Eventually, the world will run out of oil. We call resources like oil **non-renewable resources.** Once they are gone, we can't renew them.

Other examples of non-renewable resources are minerals,

such as copper and gold. There is only so much copper or gold in the world. We can't create or grow any more.

Growing More Resources

Paper bags come from trees. We cut down the trees, chop them into small pieces, and mix the pieces with water and chemicals to make pulp. The pulp is turned into paper, and the paper is made into bags.

Trees are a natural resource, like oil. But unlike oil, we can grow more trees. Therefore, trees are a **renewable resource**. If looked after properly, they need never run out.

Water is another example of a renewable resource. Rain falls from the sky into the rivers and streams, and flows out to the ocean. It evaporates back into the clouds, then falls again as rain. It is a never-ending cycle.

Making Your Choice

Let's go back to your decision about which kind of bag to choose at the store. You might decide to use paper bags because they come from a renewable resource. We can always grow more trees and make more paper.

However, think about the fact that it takes a long time for a tree to grow. Today, loggers are cutting down trees that took hundreds of years to grow. Even if we replace the trees we cut down, we will have to wait a long time for them to grow big enough to use.

Forests are also valuable for reasons other than making paper bags. Trees are sometimes called the "lungs of the earth." They produce the oxygen that we need to breathe. They also provide shade and keep many parts of the world from being too hot. As well, forests provide a home for many kinds of birds and animals. Without the forests, these creatures might disappear.

Forests produce more than trees. Maple syrup is produced from the sap of the maple tree. Each year, Canada produces three-quarters of all the maple syrup in the world. Have you ever been to a sugaring off, where maple syrup is made?

Sap from maple trees is gathered in small buckets. In the last 20 years, air pollution has killed many trees, causing a decrease in the amount of maple syrup that Canada produces.

The spotted owl lives in the old forests along the Pacific Coast. As more and more of this forest is cut down by loggers, the spotted owl is in danger of disappearing. People who care about the owl want the logging to stop. But loggers worry about their jobs disappearing. These are difficult choices.

Try This

Here is a list of natural resources:

- coal

- water

- gasoline

- fish

- fur

- copper

- land

Write down these resources. Can you think of any others to add to the list? Next to each resource, indicate whether it is renewable or non-renewable.

Think For Yourself

A **log** is a detailed record of things that are done or that happen.

Use a **log** like this one to keep track of all the things your family uses and throws away in a week Some examples might be newspapers and soft-drink cans. For each product, suggest an alternative—something else that you could use or do instead. For instance, instead of buying a newspaper, you could get your news from television or on the Internet.

Day	Items	Amount	Alternative
Monday	newspaper	1	radio news
	milk carton	2	glass bottles
	egg carton	1	reuse the carton
	paper napkins	5	container
	plastic sandwich bag	2	reuse the bag

At the end of the week, examine your log. In each case, note whether the item is made from a renewable or non-renewable resource. What are the advantages of using the alternative item?

One way to recycle is to put food scraps in a compost bin.

The Forest Industry in British Columbia

Paper bags are only one of many products that are made from wood. In your classroom alone, you can probably identify several more products, from the paper that you write on to the wooden table and chairs in the corner.

Because we use so many things made from wood, the forest industry has long been one of the most important industries in British Columbia.

Aboriginal Peoples and the Forests

From earliest times, the Aboriginal peoples used wood to make many different products. They built their houses out of cedar planks. They made dugout canoes from the trunks of the trees, and carved the paddles as well.

Their clothing came from the bark of trees. They used the roots to make fish nets and rope. Today, Aboriginal artists still use wood to carve their totem poles and masks.

Aboriginal peoples relied on the forest, but they didn't use large quantities of wood. They only cut down enough for their own use. With their stones tools, they weren't able to lay waste to an entire forest, even if they had wanted to. Furthermore, there weren't as many people as there are now.

Aboriginal peoples believed they had a connection to every living thing, including the trees. Many of their traditions and beliefs are about respecting and preserving the natural world. As a result, they didn't put the forests at risk.

Logging Begins

The earliest Europeans in British Columbia admired the thick forests of tall timber. They began cutting down trees to use as masts on their sailing ships. As more and more people came to live in the province, they built sawmills to cut lumber for houses. Lumber from British Columbia was shipped to California, Hawaii, and Australia.

Logging began along the coast, where the trees were easy to reach. Using axes and handsaws, loggers felled the trees on the steep slopes and slid the logs into the water. They were called handloggers because they did all the work by hand. There was no machinery to help them.

The loggers tied the floating logs together into booms, which were towed to the nearest sawmill to be cut up into lumber.

Machinery in the Woods

As more settlers moved to British Columbia, they needed more places to live. They also needed more places to grow crops to feed themselves. They cleared the forest and built towns and farms. Trees were used to build houses, hotels, and stores. Wood was burned as a fuel.

Once the railway came west, British Columbia grew rapidly. The loggers could now go deeper into the forest to cut down the trees, using the trains to haul the logs back to the mills. The railway also connected British Columbia to the Canadian prairie, where many new immigrants were coming to take up farms. These newcomers created a huge demand for wood to build their homes.

The railway was just one of the new machines that changed the forest industry after 1900. Loggers also used steam engines to haul the logs out of the woods. The first power saws came into use, along with bulldozers and big cranes for loading the heavy logs.

British Columbia began supplying wood to customers around the world.

The loggers look very small next to the giant cedar trees. It took hours for these two loggers to cut down a tree using their hand tools. What difference would power tools make?

Working in the Woods Today

New machines have greatly changed the forest industry. Today's loggers use chainsaws or big machines called grapple yarders to cut down trees. Trucks go deep into the forest on roads built by the forest companies to bring out logs. Helicopters are sometimes used to get to places no one used to be able to reach.

All this machinery has allowed the industry to cut more wood than ever before. Huge areas of forest have been cut down, leaving giant scars on the landscape. This process is called **clear-cutting.** Clear-cutting has caused much disagreement because it leaves such an ugly mark and is so destructive to the forest.

On the other hand, the forest industry now replaces the trees that it cuts down. People realize that we have to plant new trees if British Columbia is going to have forests in the future.

This big machine was called a steam donkey. It was a steam engine that turned the winches that pulled the cables in and out. When a tree was cut down, the cables were attached to the log. The donkey hauled the log to a central collection area.

Today, grapple yarders are used to haul logs to a landing.

Find Out

Logging is an important industry for many communities in British Columbia. If less logging goes on, people might lose jobs, and communities might lose businesses and income. On the other hand, many people worry that logging is destroying the valuable forest.

Divide into three groups. Each group can play a different role in the debate about logging. One group can take the point of view of a logger. A second group can take the point of view of someone who wants to preserve the forest. A third group can take the point of view of the mayor of a logging community.

Each group does research on its point of view about the logging industry. Each group member can try a different source of information, such as newspapers, magazines, books, and the Internet.

In your group, discuss the importance of logging. Make a list of the advantages that logging brings to your group. Are there any disadvantages? List them as well. What would be the impact of less logging? Each group should organize its ideas in a chart.

Advantages	Disadvantages	Results of Less Logging

Now compare your findings with those of the other groups. Do the groups agree? If you disagree, can you find ways of reaching a **compromise**?

In a **compromise** [KOM-pruh-mize], a dispute is settled because all sides have accepted less than they asked for.

The Three Rs

Years ago people used to joke about learning the Three Rs in school: reading, 'riting, and 'rithmetic. Of course, not all of these words start with *r*. But reading, writing, and arithmetic were considered the keys to a good education.

Nowadays people talk about a different set of Three Rs:

Reduce

Reuse

Recycle

Most Canadian communities have set up "blue box" or "blue bag" programs.

Finding a New Way

These Three Rs refer to a new way of living in the world. Throughout history, people didn't give much thought to the ways they were changing the natural world. They cut down trees, used up resources, and filled the air with pollution. They left the world to look after itself.

Today, we know that the way we live has a direct impact on the world around us. Resources don't last forever. The earth is fragile. We can't go on damaging the world we live in. We have to find a new way.

The new way is summed up by the Three Rs.

Reduce. When we reduce what we use, then we devour fewer of the world's resources. When we walk to the store instead of asking for a drive, we are reducing the need for gasoline. (And we're getting some healthy exercise!) When we turn out the lights at home when they're not needed, we are reducing the need for electricity.

Reuse.   Of course, many things we *have* to buy. We need clothes, food, books, furniture, and a lot of other things. This is where reuse comes in. When we wear the sweater that is too small for a brother or sister, we are reusing. When we keep using the same water bottle over and over, we are reusing.

Recycle. When products wear out, or we no longer need them, it's time to recycle. Recycling means that instead of being thrown away, used products are made into new ones again. Many communities collect old newspapers and use them to make new paper. Other communities have "blue boxes" where they collect bottles and cans for recycling into new products. Many businesses are now packaging their products in containers that can be used again. Can you think of other examples of recycling in your community?

A street sale is a good way to give a "second life" to your used possessions.

Try This

From your learning, name two ways in which humans are harming the natural environment. Explain how each of the Three Rs might help to improve the situation.

This bar graph shows the amount of garbage created every year in several different countries. The figures down the left-hand side are the number of kilograms *each person* throws away every year. According to the chart, each Canadian throws away about 600 kilograms of garbage. Which country throws away the most?

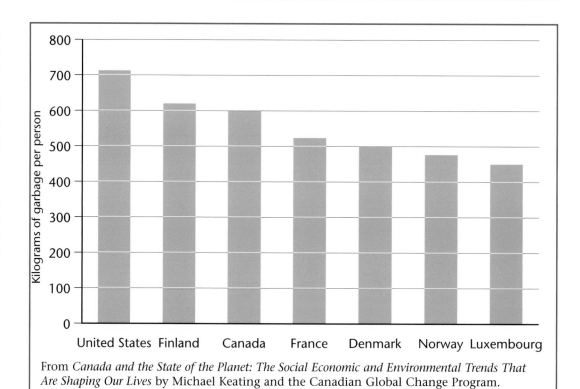

From *Canada and the State of the Planet: The Social Economic and Environmental Trends That Are Shaping Our Lives* by Michael Keating and the Canadian Global Change Program. Copyright © The Royal Society of Canada, 1997. Reprinted by permission of Oxford University Press Canada.

North Americans produce enough garbage every year to fill 70 000 garbage trucks. If they lined up bumper-to-bumper, the trucks would reach halfway to the moon!

Putting Your Ideas into Practice

When you practise the Three Rs, you are making a difference in your community.

- Fewer natural resources are needed to make new products. This means that there is less mining and less drilling for oil, and fewer trees are cut down.

- Fewer things are being thrown into the garbage, so our garbage dumps aren't being filled so quickly.

The idea of the Three Rs is to take as little as possible and, where possible, to put back as much as we can.

We are all citizens of the world. We must take care of it. The world *is* a very big place, but we all live in communities, and those are good places to start. By practising the Three Rs in your community, you can make a difference.

North Americans are among the greatest producers of waste. On average, each of us produces about 2270 kilograms of various kinds of waste each year.

Litter can take anywhere from a few weeks to thousands of years to decay. A traffic ticket takes about two weeks to decay; a wool sock, one year; an aluminum can, 200 to 500 years; and a glass bottle, an indefinite period of time.

From the Web site of the Recycling Council of Ontario.

Throwing away an aluminum soft-drink can wastes as much energy as pouring out a half-filled can of gasoline. Recycling one soft-drink can saves enough energy to run a television for three hours.

From the Web site of the Recycling Council of Ontario.

A Closer Look

Recycling

North Vancouver. The students at Deep Cove's Sherwood Park elementary school are developing a recycling project that organizers say is the only one of its kind on the North Shore.

With teaching and support from North Shore Recycling, the children are recycling everything they can get their hands on, including glass, plastic, mixed paper, clothing, textiles, and cardboard.

"They're using everything that's available to recycle," said program co-ordinator Laurie Atkinson. "They love it. They're even going home and telling their parents they [the parents] can do this, and they can't do that."

Garbage-free lunches are one of the goals set by the children. The school also hopes to sponsor a recycling poster competition.

Adapted from "Students Start Recycling Project," *The Vancouver Sun*, 29 April 1998.

Think For Yourself

Perhaps your own community has a recycling program like the one at Sherwood Park. If so, think about ways your own class can get involved.

You might send out teams of "garbage scroungers" to rescue bottles and cans from trash barrels. When they are sorted, you can turn them in for recycling. Do the cafés and restaurants in your community recycle their newspapers? What about the bus station and other public places where people sometimes leave their newspapers? Perhaps you could arrange to collect the papers for recycling.

You can keep your community clean by collecting old bottles, cans, and papers. They may even be worth some money!

Try This

Every year, on April 22nd, people all over the world celebrate Earth Day. On this day, we focus our attention on the problems facing the natural world. And we think about ways of solving these problems in our everyday lives.

One way is to think about reusing things in your home. Here are some things you could do:

- Take your own shopping bag to the store to carry things home.

- Use cloth napkins instead of paper ones.

- Buy recycled paper for your school supplies.

- Hold a street sale so that neighbours can exchange things instead of buying new ones.

You'll have many ideas of your own about how to put the Three Rs into action. Add them to the list above.

Share one new idea with a partner. Explain how you think your idea will help to preserve resources. Discuss the idea with your partner and decide if it's workable. Now it's your partner's turn to share an idea with you.

To find out more about Earth Day, visit the Earth Day Canada Web site at www.earthday.ca.

Looking Back

In this chapter, you learned about the difference between renewable and non-renewable resources. You also looked at the importance and impact of the forest industry in British Columbia.

In your everyday life, what can you do to make the world a better place?

Index

Numbers in **boldface** indicate an illustration.

A

Aboriginal peoples:
    and forests, 188
    and gold prospectors, 148
    and salmon, 158, 164, 165
    assimilation, 89, 94
    comparison chart, 21
    Dakelh, 144–145
    Elders, 84
    European influence, 19, 84–95,
      146
    government, 83–84, 96–98
    Indian Act, 89–90
    Indian name origin, 19
    masks, 90–91, **91**
    national achievement awards, 22
    Nuu-chah-nulth, 17, 86–87, **87**
    oral culture, 94, 95
    original inhabitants, 17, **83**, **146**
    potlatches, 94–95
    reserves, 85, 90
    residential schools, 91–93, **93**
    rights, 85
    self-government, 96–98
    today, 22, 96
    Tommy Prince, 57
    traditions, 86
    treaties, 85
    see also First Nations, Inuit,
      Métis
Aglukark, Susan, **22**
American Civil War, 39
American immigrants, 35
American Revolution, 35, 36, 38
Anderson, Nils, 7
Asian peoples, 41–44
    Chinese, 41–44, **42–43**, 76, 124,
      124, 160
    Indian, 41, 43, 76
    Japanese, 41, 43, 76

B

    prejudice, 42–43
    voting, 43, 76

Barker, Billy, 150, **150**
Barkerville, 148, **149**, 150,
    151–152
bartering, 141–142, **142**
Bell, John Kim, 22
Benotti, Nicole, 103
Bering Strait, 17, **19**
bias, 131–132
bilingualism, 23
Black people:
    African Rifles, 40
    slavery, 38–39
    today, 40, **40**
    underground railroad, 38, 39, **39**
Bondar, Roberta, 56, **56**
British North America Act, 79
British people:
    heritage, 31, **31**
    immigrants, 30
    Queen Elizabeth II, 29, **29**
    Seven Years War, 30

C

Canadian Constitution, 79–80
canneries, 158–161, **159**
Cariboo, 148–150, **149**, **150**, 151
Carr, Emily, 14, **14**
census, 10, 12
Charron, Théophile, 171, 172
Charter of Rights and Freedoms,
    79–80
children working, 160, **170**,
    171–172
Chinese people:
    cannery workers, 160
    Chinatowns, 41–42

David Lam, 44, **44**
head tax, 43
humiliation day, 43
immigrants, 41–44, **42–43**
prejudice, 42–43
railway workers, **42–43**, 124,
    124
voting rights, 43, 76
cities:
    air pollution, 138, 180–181,
      185
    urban problems, 179–180
    using resources, 181–182
    Vancouver port, 176–177, **176**
    world's largest, 180
citizenship, 50–53
clear-cutting, 190
communications:
    bias, 131–132
    early methods, 128–129
    forms of, 127–130
    media, 130
communities:
    cities, 175–182
    defined, 99
    fishing, 163–164
    history of, 112
    how they get named, 62
    industrial revolution, 168–173
    jobs, 111
    living together in, 48–49
    local businesses, 105
    location of, 110–111
    military defence, 110
    Powell River, 103–105, 108
    reasons for settling, 100, 104
    transportation, 110–111
    types, **101–102**
    walking tour of yours, 70
    why do certain ones thrive,
      151–152
Connolly, Amelia, **144**
Constitution, 79–80
council, 72

Photo Credits

p. 4   (tl) Al Harvey, (bl) Barrett & MacKay, (tr) V. Whelan/Valan Photos;

p. 5   (t) V. Last/Geographical Visual Aids, (b) Joseph R. Pearce/Valan Photos;

p. 7   Lois Anderson;

p. 9   Department of Immigration and Citizenship, Government of Canada;

p. 10   Stone/Elie Bernager;

p. 13   *The Solemn Land* by J.E.H. MacDonald, 1921, oil on canvas, National Gallery of Canada, Ottawa;

p. 14   (t) D-06009/British Columbia Archives, (b) *Big Raven* by Emily Carr, oil on canvas. Photo by Trevor Mills/Vancouver Art Gallery;

p. 18   Courtesy UBC Museum of Anthropology, Vancouver, Canada;

p. 20   National Archives of Canada/ NAC C-46498;

p. 22   Pool-Shaun Best/CP Photo;

p. 23   Kevork Djansezian/AP Photo;

p. 25   National Archives of Canada/NAC C-866;

p. 26   National Archives of Canada/NAC C-2634;

p. 27   *A View of the Chateau-Richer, Cape Torment and Lower End of the Isle of Orleans* by Thomas Davies, 1787, National Gallery of Canada, Ottawa;

p. 28   Barrett & MacKay;

p. 29   Dick Hemingway;

p. 31   Cylla von Tiedmann/Stratford Festival;

p. 34   93.049P/2828 The United Church of Canada/Victoria University Archives, Toronto;

p. 39   Bettmann-CORBIS;

p. 40   Dick Hemingway;

p. 42   72553/British Columbia Archives;

p. 44   John Thompson/The Province;

p. 45   Annie Griffiths Belt/CORBIS;

p. 49   Al Harvey;

p. 50   Ryan Remiorz/CP Photo;

p. 52   Toronto Star/Millar;

p. 53   J. Merrithew/Ivy Images;

p. 54   CP Photo;

p. 56   (t) Courtesy of The Governor General of Canada, (b) NASA;

p. 57   (t) Provincial Archives of Manitoba/N197, (b) CP Photo;

p. 59   Dave Sandford/Hockey Hall of Fame;

p. 65   L. Thomas/Ivy Images;

p. 68   D.R.S. Loveridge/Valan Photos;

p. 73   Reproduced with the consent of the Library of Parliament;

p. 75   Carlo Allegri/National Post;

p. 76   C. Jessop/CP Photo;

p. 78   Free the Children;

p. 80   Reproduced with the permission of the Minister of Public Works and Government Services, Canada, 2000;

p. 83   F-088990/Walter Forrest Montgomery/British Columbia Archives;

p. 84   Eastcott/Momatiuk/Valan Photos;

p. 88   Jeff Foott/Valan Photos;

p. 91   PDP02056/British Columbia Archives;

p. 93   Sessional Papers #14, Department of Indian Affairs/Metropolitan Toronto Reference Library;

p. 97   Courtesy of Rosemarie Kuptana;

p. 101   (t) *Tracks and Traffic, 1912*, oil on canvas, Art Gallery of Ontario, Toronto Gift of Walter C. Laidlaw, 1937, (m) MacDougal/First Light, (b) *Silver Plains, Manitoba, 1930*, by Walter J. Phillips, watercolour, National Gallery of Canada, Ottawa;

p. 102   (t) John Sylvester Photography, (m) *Cobalt* by Yvonne McKague Housser, 1931, oil on canvas, National Gallery of Canada, Ottawa, (b) Gordon Miller;

p. 104   Kim Stallknecht/Ivy Images;

p. 109   Phillip Norton/Valan Photos;

p. 111   *Citadel of Quebec City*, watercolour, by P.J. Bainbridge, © Royal Ontario Museum;

p. 112   Charlene Daley/Valan Photos;

p. 116   (t) Photograph courtesy of the Maritime Museum of the Atlantic, Halifax, Nova Scotia, Canada, (b) *The Canadian Southern Railway at Niagara*, 1870, oil on canvas, National Gallery of Canada, Ottawa;

p. 117   (t) Metropolitan Reference Library/J. Ross Robertson Collection, MTL2284, (m) Denis Roy/Valan Photos, (b) National Archives of Canada/NAC C-2774;

p. 118   S. Rossotto/First Light;

p. 119   National Archives of Canada/NAC PA-145428;

p. 121   R. Cote/Ponopresse;

p. 123   National Archives of Canada/NAC C-14115;

p. 124   R-B1789/Saskatchewan Archives;

p. 135   (tl) V. Whelan/Valan Photos, (bl) Francis Lepine/Valan Photos, (tr) Tom W. Parkin/Valan Photos, (br) Eastcott/Momatiur/Valan Photos;

p. 139   Ballard Fuel Systems;

p. 140   Jeff Foott/Valan Photos;

p. 144   (l) Hudson's Bay Company Archives, Provincial Archives of Manitoba, (r) H004909/British Columbia Archives;

p. 145   National Archives of Canada/NAC C-3676;

p. 147   PDP-02612/British Columbia Archives;

p. 149   National Archives of Canada/C-8077;

p. 150   (t) A-01144/British Columbia Archives, (b) A-00353/British Columbia Archives;

p. 155   Vancouver Sun;

p. 159   (t) CVA 586-972 Don Coltman/Steffens-Colmer Studio/City of Vancouver Archives, (b) British Columbia Archives;

p. 161   C-08018/British Columbia Archives;

p. 162   Museum of Flight/CORBIS;

p. 163   Al Harvey;

p. 168   Metropolitan Toronto Reference Library/J. Ross Robertson Collection, MTL 2720;

p. 169   (l) National Archives of Canada/NAC C-8827, (r) National Archives of Canada/NAC C-18734;

p. 170   Lewis W. Hine/CORBIS;

p. 173   N12314 Winnipeg Strike 26/Provincial Archives of Manitoba;

p. 176   Gunter Marx/CORBIS;

p. 177   Al Harvey;

p. 179   Ottmar Bierwagen/Ivy Images;

p. 180   Y.R. Tymstra/Valan Photos;

p. 184   Wouterloot-Gregoire/Valan Photos;

p. 186   Robert Lankinen/First Light;

p. 189   F-9180/British Columbia Archives;

p. 190   (t) CORBIS, (b) Thomas Kitchin/First Light;

p. 192   Dick Hemingway;

p. 195   Tom W. Parkin/Valan Photos;

p. 196   Glenn Baglo/Vancouver Sun.

Every effort has been made to trace the original source of material and photographs contained in this book. Where the attempt has been unsuccessful, the publisher would be pleased to hear from copyright holders to rectify any ommisions.